KRAUTROCK

COSMIC ROCK AND ITS LEGACY

black dog
publishing
london uk

CONTENTS

INTRODU

David Stubbs

The moniker "Krautrock" was slapped on the experimental German rock movement of the late 1960s and early 1970s by the British music press, and ironically retained by its practitioners. It reflected the condescension of the Anglo-American orientated rock establishment, who found the very fact that these groups were German inherently amusing and could no more imagine that the citizens of this vanquished nation, with their unmusical, *umlaut*-ridden language and pidgin take on rock mores were capable of making any sort of significant contribution to popular music. To have suggested otherwise would be like arguing that there was a rich, undiscovered seam of German situation comedy well worth investigating. Instead, in the UK and America, they continued to worship at the altar of Jethro Tull, Deep Purple, Pink Floyd, The Eagles, who, in contrast to these strange,

droning, synthesizer-obsessed Teutons, were worthy, important and serious musicians, whose music was 'progressing' somewhere or other.

Even as it was at its raging, droning, kosmische height, Krautrock was regarded as a continental eccentricity. Perhaps the first group to break into the collective Anglo-American consciousness were Kraftwerk, who in 1975 had a hit with "Autobahn", which obliquely parodied The Beach Boys and paid serene homage to Germany's motorway system. That same year, they also featured on the UK show Tomorrow's World, which speculated with mixed results as to what the future would be like in the 1980s, 1990s and beyond. Dressed like civil servants, bashing away on pieces of wired up metal, chanting effetely in their own tongue and twiddling buttons in lieu of proper instruments with fretboards, they seemed to have as much

1 German autobahn, 1935.

2 A torn-down Berlin after the Second World War, 1945.
© bpk/Carl Weirother.

3 A US soldier in denazification Germany.

CTION

to do with rock'n'roll as a briefcase. As Kraftwerk's Florian Schneider leered to camera in what appeared to be a German version of a smile, the slightly stunned Tomorrow's World voice-over informed us that Kraftwerk were looking to dispense with instruments altogether and create special suits with electronic buttons sewn into their lapels. Well, *natürlich*. There had been a spate of novelty synthesizer hits during the 1970s and "Autobahn" appeared to merely be the latest, to be junked alongside Rolf Harris' Stylophone by posterity, unlikely to stand the test of time like Barclay James Harvest.

Tomorrow's World called correctly, if a little quizzically, on Kraftwerk. However, it was not alone in failing to grasp the extent to which home-grown German rock music of the 1960s and 1970s would not just merely hold its own as a going concern but provide an eternally luminous

touchstone for late twentieth and twenty-first century rock and dance music, even going so far as to reconfigure the very nature of popular music itself. By the late 1970s, Krautrock was pretty much dead, but its potent afterlife was only just about to begin.

It was no coincidence that Germany should play host to a rock revolution. Razed to the ground by the Second World War, it was a nation whose slate had been wiped effectively clean. Almost immediately, in the late 1940s and early 1950s, musical theorists and practitioners like Herbert Eimert and Karlheinz Stockhausen dreamt and attempted to conceive of a wholly new music in the recently born medium of electronics, a music which, unlike the French conception of *musique concrète* (a music based on manipulations of taped found sounds) was sourced entirely from the new machinery, absolute in its purity

4

and originality and untainted by the terrible after-stench of a fallen world.

Of course, such experimentalism made no headway with the German public. Despite attempts at denazification programmes, there was no great wave of remorse among the German people for the crimes perpetrated by them or in their name. Such a change of mindset was impossible to engender overnight, and it was only with the inducement of dollars from the Marshall Plan that Germans felt able to rebuild a civil society in which the Third Reich was merely unmentioned, rather than atoned for. A new civic stratum of lawyers, teachers, professors, politicians and so forth was drawn from the ranks of those who had once been ardent supporters of Hitler but who now laboured into the 1950s under a dull cloud of collective, affected amnesia.

Meanwhile, the presence of British and American soldiers in Germany meant that the country subsisted on the imported rhythms of Anglo-American rock, pop, soul, jazz and R&B. Many musicians, such as Tangerine Dream's Edgar Froese, who would later become Krautrock pioneers, cut their teeth playing in dance bands playing covers. The Anglo-American influence was not entirely inane, while the hunger of younger German audiences for a music with an incandescent futurebeat was fierce indeed. It was in Hamburg that The Beatles came alive as a band, urged nightly by the owner of a club in Reeperbahn, Hamburg, to "Mach schau!" ("Make a show"). The Monks, an American, German-based group, would also light fires in the heads of those who witnessed them. However, it was with the advent of hippiedom, and the countercultural dissent that was

4 Spirits of Sound, 1966. From left to right: Uwe Frisch, Ralph
Ermisch, Michael Rother. Courtesy Michael Rother.

5 Floh de Cologne. Courtesy Eurock Archives.

6 The murdered body of Benno Ohnesorg, Berlin, 1967.
© bpk/Axel Benzmann.

7 Poster for an exhibition on the political opposition in West
Germany, 1967. Courtesy Deutsches Plakat Museum.
Photo: Jens Nober.

5

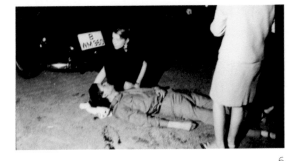

6

Politische
Opposition
in der
Bundesrepublik

Dokumente, Bilder, Bücher
Zeichnungen von Carlo Schellemann
Eröffnung mit Yaak Karsunke
und Wolf Brannasky.
19. April, 20 Uhr
Ausstellung: 20. 4.–4. 6. 1968
Stadtbücherei Nürnberg
Gewerbemuseumsplatz 4

7

fomenting in campuses across Europe in the
1960s that the seeds of Krautrock were sewn,
especially following the death of the student
Benno Ohnesorg in June 1967. This event was a
catalyst for a generation increasingly angered
at their immediate elders whom they regarded
as quietly complicit in war crimes and the
downfall of Germany, a generation increasingly
politicised and galvanised by the radicalism,
both musical and political, of young America,
as well as the freedom and affluence that that
country represented.

The German generation entering adulthood in
the late 1960s, unborn in 1945, was the first
to be untouched by the war, and the first able
to look back in disgust and forward with hope.
A wave of radicalism swept through the arts,
cinema (with figures like Werner Herzog), and
·politics, from the *Sozialistische Deutsche*

Studentenbund (SDS) to the Red Army Faction,
and into music.

The relationship between Krautrock and Anglo-
American music was paradoxical. On the one
hand, it was hugely influential. Irmin Schmidt
and Holger Czukay formed Can as a result of
being played new American rock music by young
guitarist Michael Karoli and from hearing at
first hand the primitive, Ur-rock of MC5 and
The Velvet Underground on visiting the States.
Kraftwerk's "Autobahn" was in part inspired by,
and pays homage to, The Beach Boys. A German
tour by The Mothers Of Invention ignited the
sort of nationwide epiphanies that The Sex
Pistols' UK tour would a decade later. Groups
like Guru Guru were deeply conscious of their
debt to Jimi Hendrix. The space rock of Pink
Floyd, as showcased live or on the live disc of
the 1969 album *Ummagumma*, shines like a moon

8

over much of Krautrock's free-form, wailing, celestial output. Captain Beefheart, the psychedelic movement in general (Timothy Leary eventually fetched up in Germany and made an album with Ash Ra Tempel) were also a vital resource in shaping and colouring in the new movement.

However, there was about Krautrock a deferred desire to rebuild, to begin again, one which would take almost a quarter of a century to bear fruit. There was a sense of a generation culturally orphaned; "We had no fathers", Kraftwerk's Ralf Hütter once said. There was also a sense that, as well as providing inspiration, the Americans were also an occupying force and it was necessary to inaugurate a music that was wholly unique in origin, not out of some sense of *über alles* Aryan supremacism bit in order to re-establish

a shattered self-identity. It was, in short, the perfect breeding ground for a new avant-garde. In this respect, Stockhausen, composer of such electronic masterpieces as *Kontakte, Hymnen* and *Gesang Der Jünglinge*, shone a light from across the dark generation gap. Ralf Hütter was an avid fan of his, while Can's Holger Czukay had been his pupil.

Krautrock's breeding grounds were sound/arts labs, complexes and compounds, set apart from regular civic and cultural life, places where musicians could return, undistracted, to a new set of first principles of their own—places like Berlin's Zodiak Free Arts Lab, where painter-turned-(non) musician Conrad Schnitzler and Klaus Schulze first made waves. Faust, sold to Polydor as a "new Beatles" by their wily manager set up at Wümme, in a converted former school building, Can at Schloss Nörvenich outside

9

8 Mothers of Invention German tour poster by Günther Kieser, 1968. Courtesy Deutsches Plakat Museum. Photo: Jens Nober.

9 Faust at Wümme. Courtesy Andy Wilson/faust-pages.com.

10 Can with Damo Suzuki at Schloss Nörvenich. Courtesy Spoon Records.

11 Timothy Leary with his daughter, grandchild and Brian Barritt, shortly after his arrival in Switzerland, 1971. Courtesy Brian Barritt.

Cologne, Kraftwerk in their Kling Klang studios in Düsseldorf.

Each in their different way was set upon assembling an entirely new music from the fragments of the past and the tools of the future. Faust's debut album, Dada-like in its collage and spliced juxtaposition of unlikely musical elements and interventions, begins with 'samples' of The Rolling Stones and The Beatles immolated and blasted in a dirty conflagration of untamed electronics. Can played furiously and introvertedly away into inner space as if jamming their way back to a mythical pre-history of rock, subject to sudden changes of direction by bassist Czukay and keyboardist Schmidt, the sort of invisible signals which cause birds to rocket for no apparent reason. Klaus Dinger, drummer of NEU! meanwhile, would posit an alternative, rhythmical pattern with his 'motorik' beat, duly praised by Brian Eno, who said that "there were three great beats in the '70s: Fela Kuti's Afrobeat, James Brown's funk and Klaus Dinger's NEU!-beat."

And then, there were Kraftwerk, whose later works some Krautrock purists tend to shy away from, as if they were an opportunistic departure from the true spirit of the genre, yet who effected the greatest alterations in the international grid of popular music of all. Initially, they were as hirsute and hippyish and apt to lengthy flute solos as any of their peers. However, it was their decision to crop their hair, restrict themselves exclusively to electronic instruments and posit a disingenuously serene relationship between man and technology which was calculated to raise the hackles of the more bucolic, idealistic, longhair wing of the Krautrock movement. They were a camp,

13 A very early Kraftwerk. From left to right: Houschäng
Néjadepour, Klaus Dinger, Florian Schneider, Eberhard
Kranemann, 1971. Courtesy Eberhard Kranemann.
14 Brian Eno with Harmonia, 1976. © Harmonia 76.
Photo: Christine Roedelius.
15 Kraftwerk in Keystone Club, California, during their
first US tour, early 1980s. Courtesy Eurock Archives.
Photo: Archie Patterson

14

13

seemingly deliberate affront to all that rock, from left to right field, was supposed to stand for. In rejecting the guitar, they had deliberately emasculated themselves, in posing in suits they were deliberately re-entering the ranks of the bourgeoisie. They hummed sweetly and uncritically about the German motorway network Hitler had established, but in so doing reclaimed the very roads themselves from the Nazis. Despite their futuristic reputation they did not seek escape in the cosmos but enabled in their pretty melodies and girder-like rhythms practical resolution here on earth, between past and present and future, station to station, metal on metal. David Bowie was among the first to embrace and absorb Kraftwerk, to get them. Bowie had lent the scene credibility and exposure when he relocated from America to Berlin in 1976, as if anticipating a continental

shift, for his "Berlin" period, during which time he and Kraftwerk name-checked one another on their albums. Bowie reinfused his career and profile with Krautrock blood. But within the next few years they would be generally vindicated, Krautrock's ultimate success story. They are the acknowledged forefathers of UK synthpop and techno, with Afrika Bambaata using their "Trans-Europe Express" as the chassis for a freshly electrified hip hop scene in 1982. Kraftwerk's influence ran like cable through subsequent pop history on both sides of the Atlantic. By 1986, with the electrification of pop pretty much complete, they effectively withdrew, their work done, a trans-European, trans-American transformation brought about on a colossal scale. Today, due homage is paid to Kraftwerk, despite their own reclusiveness. When Chris Martin of Coldplay sought permission to

15

use the melody of Kraftwerk's "Computer Love" on one of their hits, his superstar status did not overly impress the group. After weeks of indirect contact with Kraftwerk via lawyers, he eventually received a single, one-word message by way of permission: "yes".

That said, the more pervasive and profound influence of Krautrock has been more insinuating and indirect. It wasn't just NEU! who impressed Brian Eno—Cluster's gentle mid-period, their deceptively slight watercolour instrumentals also caught his ear as he was developing his series of late 1970s ambient recordings whose impact, albeit after a 20 year delay, would eventually be enormous. It was not just Kraftwerk who prefigured later developments in dance and rave but also Can, as their 1997 remix album, *Sacrilege*, including contributions from A Guy Called Gerald, U.N.K.L.E and System

7, attested. Can's own "Moonshake", released as early as 1973, is like a prototype example of robo-dance music. The first wave of UK post-punk was populated with Krautrock students, including The Buzzcocks' Pete Shelley, The Fall's Mark E Smith, John Lydon and Julian Cope, whose 1980s history of Krautrock helped kick in a fresh wave of fascination for all good things 1970's and Teutonic. Krautrock was one of the genres very pointedly exempt from punk's scathing iconoclasm. A further wave of German groups born in the 1980s, including DAF and Einstürzende Neubauten, helped reinforce the notion that new relationships between melody and drone, order and chaos, electronics and raw noise, rhythm and vocals, could lead to new forms that didn't merely obediently rehash the forefathers of classic rock. On tracks like "Der Mussolini", DAF stripped back

16 Michael Karoli (left) and Irmin Schmidt (right), Can. Courtesy Spoon Records.

17

the electropop model established by Kraftwerk and created from a new Point Zero a bolder, more powerful, synthetic dancefloor upgrade, in which iron and irony melded. As for Neubauten, their name, which translated as "Collapsing New Buildings", was indicative of a sound reassembled from recently buckled mortar and girders, as if they had suffered an equivalent post-war collapse of their own. They took up where Faust had left off on "Mamie Is Blue". From the 1990s onwards, the likes of Basic Channel and the Kompakt label took up the baton of what had become a sleek, established tradition of German innovation.

Today, as the original generations of Krautrockers grow elderly, their influence has intensified rather than dimmed. It is a fresh well of coloured liquid, with old works by less obvious artists like Guru Guru and Achim Reichel reissued, rediscovered and reappraised by a new wave of musicians and sound artists hungry for futures past. From San Francisco to Tokyo, a vast new generation of droneheads, post rockers, electronic minimalists and acid friend experimentalists disenfranchised by the market-driven, neo-conservative aridity of mainstream popular music have cast back to 1970s Germany for inspiration. Krautrock's space guitars, pealing electronics, endless repetitions and cyclical percussion, wailing out into infinite inner and outer space all those decades ago speaks directly to us today, having gone over the heads of the vast, vast majority of their own contemporaries. The lofty prog rockers of the early 1970s, who imagined that their own, mock-symphonic edifices would stand like cathedrals down the ages would be dismayed to see that relatively little use is made of their

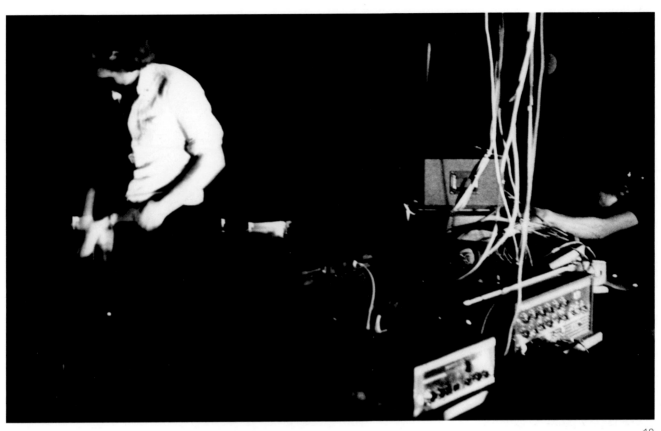

18

17 Mani Neumeier of Guru Guru. Courtesy Eurock Archives.
18 Conrad Schnitzler with Tangerine Dream at the Zodiak Free
Arts Lab. Courtesy Wolfgang Seidel. Photo: Werner Strey.

works nowadays. Few serious people are taking their cue from Genesis.

Krautrock was about cultural self-reassertion, an implicit attempt to be free of both the dark past of their immediate forefathers and a determination to create a new musical autonomy, a homegrown music which took its cue from Britain and America but was not utterly dependent or absolutely subsidised by its culturally overbearing allies. In the process, it reinvented pop music—via David Bowie, via hip hop, via ambient and electronica—and carries on with that process of reinvention and permutation, today and tomorrow. The proof of it isn't it obvious nods like that delivered by Coldplay. Krautrock isn't honoured by people merely apeing it or lazily referencing it, though there is a good deal of that about. Rather, the influence of Krautrock is best felt in those artists who

choose to throw out old templates, return to absolute beginnings in order to quickly arrive at more inventive ends. So, for example, while all of minimal techno owes its origins to Kraftwerk, it arrives at permutations undreamt of by Ralf Hütter, Florian Schneider et al. The Krautrock influence is felt depressingly little in twenty-first century mainstream guitar rock, conservative and compressed, but in the more "unfinished", open-ended, commercially peripheral likes of post-rock artists ranging from the neo-psychedelia merchants Loop through to Tortoise, LaBradford, Yo La Tengo, Animal Collective, Battles, and Alex Delivery among others, who, in playing as if music were a blank canvas upon which they are splashing the first strokes of paint, show clearly that they have in fact exposed themselves to the likes of Can and Popol Vuh somewhere back down the

INTRODUCTION 17
DAVID STUBBS

19

line. The watercolour, subversively seductive electronica of Taylor Deupree and Susumu Yokota seem unimaginable without the original example of Cluster. The tentacles of Krautrock have even extended to hip hop, as shown in Faust's 2004 collaboration with the New Jersey trio Dälek, Derbe Respect, Alder. This was perfectly appropriate—collage is as important a factor in hip hop as it is in Krautrock. The Horrors. Stereolab, Aphex Twin—cast your eye in every direction away from the centre and you'll find an abundance of neo-innovators who knowingly owe something of their impetus to the Germans. Sometimes the connections are obscure,

mediated and indirect, but Krautrock reset the rhythms, boosted the palette and blew open gaping holes into the infinite in contemporary music. It showed that you could begin anywhere, Düsseldorf even, and fetch up anywhere, miles or even aeons away, even if the methods you used—minimalism, repetition—made it feel like you weren't making any sort of "progress" at all. Even those who are unaware of the moniker Krautrock would swiftly become aware of what a dull and colourless musical world this would be were its influence to be subtracted from it. As it is, those corners where its inventions are either ignored or resisted are grey, grey indeed.

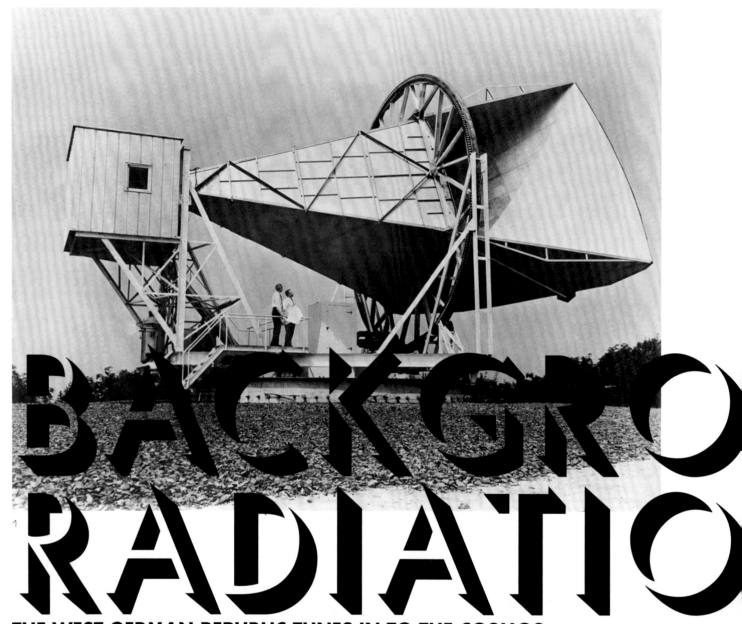

BACKGRO RADIATIO

THE WEST GERMAN REPUBLIC TUNES IN TO THE COSMOS

Ken Hollings

Not everyone makes it through to the end of Hans-Jürgen Syberberg's seven-hour *Hitler: A Film from Germany*, but most will remember how it begins. "Stars flying towards us" runs the opening direction in the published script. "A voyage into the darkness of outer space. The noise of static familiar to us from the radio of the 1930s and the opening of Mozart's Piano Concerto in D Minor." Variations on this haunting moment recur throughout Syberberg's ambitious 'work of mourning', particularly at the opening and closing to each of the film's

four main parts. The mingling of stars with radio static and classical music suggests the tragic events they relate are taking place sub specie aeternitatis, while the German director's explicit references to 1930s wireless receivers and the well-tempered piano keyboard serve as reminders that these same events are coming to us through the medium of human technology. By their agency we have allowed ourselves to be 'tuned in' to a vast cosmic drama. Completing a trilogy of films Syberberg began in 1972 with *Ludwig, Requiem*

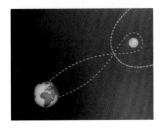
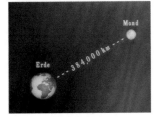

2

1 Arno Penzios and Robert Wilson with the Horn Antenna, New Jersey.

2 Film stills from Fritz Lang's *The Woman in the Moon*, 1929.

3 (Overleaf) The Volksempfänger VE-301.

UND

WIR RICHTEN ANTENNEN INS FIRMAMENT EMPFANGEN DIE TÖNE DIE NIEMAND KENNT (WE ARE AIMING ANTENNA AT THE SKY RECEIVING TONES NO ONE KNOWS)
KRAFTWERK

I AM A TRANSMITTER. I RADIATE.
JOSEPH BEUYS

for a Virgin King and continued with *Karl May* in 1974, *Hitler, a Film from Germany* appeared to be a film whose time had both come and gone. Its release coincided with the 'German Autumn' of 1977: a period of deep political unrest that saw the violent deaths of Red Army Faction members Andreas Baader, Jan Carl Raspe and Gudrun Ensslin in Stammheim prison, as well as that of kidnapped industrialist Hans-Martin Schleyer, whose body was recovered from an abandoned car in eastern France, close to the Swiss and German borders.

"Media determine our situation" Friedrich Kittler declared with military precision at the very start of his study *Gramophone, Film, Typewriter;* and Syberberg's depiction of Hitler as the dangerously unstable creation of radio voices, projected images and recorded snatches of music spoke directly to Germany that autumn in terms it could not fail to understand. Themes from Wagner's *Parsifal* and Beethoven's *Fidelio* are mixed with Goebbels' broadcast speeches and the sounds of mass rallies; a studio soundstage is heaped with cheap theatrical props and cut-out figures from *The Cabinet of Dr Caligari, Nosferatu* and *Alraune;* mannequins, ventriloquist's dummies and inflatable sex dolls share the same set as art works by Albrecht Dürer, Otto Runge and Caspar David Friedrich. By combining the immersive aesthetics of Wagner's *gesamstkunstwerk* with the stringent distancing techniques of Brecht's Epic Theatre, Syberberg offered his viewers a seven-hour meditation on Adolf Hitler as the greatest media event of the entire twentieth century. No wonder the film was greeted by audience walkouts and heated critical exchanges. Politically suspect even from the perspective of a democracy protected at gunpoint, culturally compromised in an age when culture was increasingly a reasoned debate *about* culture, Syberberg's *Hitler* seemed to exist for the very purpose of emptying cinemas by any means necessary. Under what other circumstances could duration be read as depth?

And yet we still find ourselves confronted by those stars rushing towards us through the darkness. The sound of radio static connects inner and outer space. Tuning through a wireless dial also means discovering that unique audible space which exists between stations: a mysterious zone of harmonies and distortions that function according to some strange and distinct logic of their own. As Emmanuel Kant observed in his *Critique of Practical Reason*: "Two things fill the mind with ever new and increasing admiration and awe, the more often and steadily they are reflected upon—the starry heavens above me and the moral law within me." To dream of travelling through outer space is, according to Syberberg, also to journey into the dark night of the inner self. It is this same dream that inspired Fritz Lang's last silent movie, the science-fiction adventure *The Woman in the Moon*, which Hitler later banned on the grounds that it revealed too much about Germany's own missile programme, and Wernher von Braun's self-imposed mission to build rockets first for the Nazis and then for NASA.

It is, consequently, also the dream that kept the Romantic poet Heinrich Heine awake at night, shedding hot tears over Germany's fate. He was not the only one to find his sleep troubled by this legacy. Kant's dictum about the stars above the moral law within was inscribed on his tombstone in Königsberg, better known today as Kaliningrad. The grave sustained severe damage during World War II but was later repaired, meaning that Kant's words can now be read in Russian and German.

•

To venture outwards is therefore to journey inwards as well. "I feel the air of another planet" exults the German modernist Stephan George, connecting both trajectories in one transported moment in his poem "Rapture", first published in 1907. The following year this same line was used by Arnold Schoenberg to mark the dramatic shift into atonality that occurs in the last movement of his *String Quartet No. 2*. The introductory bars leading up to it are intended by the composer to evoke the rarefied atmosphere through which the female singer is to ascend in order to reach interplanetary space. A vast new dimension suddenly opens up. "I lose myself in tones, circling, weaving", the soprano continues. "With unfathomable thanks and unnamed love, I happily surrender to the great breath."

The ether had undergone a big change by then, however. The "great breath" was alive with radio signals, some of which were already capable of conjuring up "tones circling, weaving" out of the air itself. In the same year that saw George's "Rapture" appear in print, a recording of Rossini's *William Tell* overture was broadcast from a laboratory in New York City. Although there were barely any receivers in existence at the time, this is one of the earliest known examples of such material being sent out over the airwaves. Thanks to the power of radio, music's vast new dimension was revealed to be its own invisibility. It could be everywhere and nowhere at the same time.

Like many revelations, this one is not without precedent. "You see, my son, here time turns into space" Gurnemanz announces at the end of Act One in Wagner's *Parsifal* as the Castle of the Grail magically appears before the audience's eyes. Such stage illusions often depend more upon the unseen than what is put on show. Why else would Wagner insist that the orchestra be kept out of sight in the Bayreuth Festspielhaus, where his vast cycle of operatic works was to be staged in a darkened auditorium? By fooling the spectator's senses, music's invisibility supplies the means by which the immersive *gesamstkunstwerk* can be brought into being; "under the influence of the accompanying music", Wagner remarked of *Parsifal's* transformation scene, "we were, as in a state of dreamy rapture, to be led imperceptibly along the trackless ways to the Castle of the Grail." A double proscenium stage adds to the effect, putting greater distance between members of the audience and the dreamlike scene unfolding before them.

Rapture on such a grand scale can also be dangerous. "Artists often miscalculate when they aim at a sensual effect for their works of art", Nietzsche declared in *Human, All Too Human*, having just escaped from Wagner's spell, "for their viewers or listeners no longer have all their senses about them, and, quite against the artist's intentions, arrive by means of his work of art at a 'sanctity' of feeling that is closely related to boredom." Under what other circumstances could depth be read as duration?

As music continued to bring the airwaves to life during the early decades of the twentieth century, radio's own invisible power was also becoming apparent. Arnolt Bronnen's 1935 novel *Struggle in the Ether* detailed some of the private desires and public forces that had helped bring Germany's radio networks into being. "Records, gramophones, money", a young secretary wistfully comments at one point in the narrative, "if one could sit here without records, gramophones, money, but still hear music…" Aware of the rapture that goes along with breathing the unseen air of another planet, Bronnen also notes that his fictional secretary '"smiled, lost in a dream" as she spoke these last words.

"My very first memory stems from the time when I was about three-and-a-half years old" the composer Karlheinz Stockhausen would recall at the end of the twentieth century. "My father was a school teacher and he had bought a small radio. I can still see that box in front of me… and my mother liked singing so she liked to listen to this small radio."

The radio in question would most likely have been a Volksempfanger VE-301, 'the People's Receiver'. Mass produced and relatively cheap,

3

the box-like VE-301 radio was first presented to
the public at the *Internationale Funkausstellung*
in Berlin on August 18 1933. In a speech
delivered at the exhibition that same day, Reich
Minister of Popular Enlightenment and Propaganda
Dr Joseph Goebbels praised radio as the "first and
most influential intermediary between... movement
and nation, between idea and man", indicating
the powerful link forged by means of radio's
'dreamy rapture' between the individual listener
and the social order. Popular in every sense of
the word, most models of the People's Receiver
lacked a shortwave band and were consequently
able to receive only local broadcasts: major
foreign stations weren't marked on the dial and
later versions didn't even have a tuning scale.
The Minister for Popular Enlightenment welcomed
such limitations, however. "We want a radio
that marches with the nation", he declared in
his August 18 speech, "a radio that works for
the people". The new medium had by then already
played a key role in both co-ordinating and
covering the public book burnings carried out at
universities throughout Germany just three months
previously. Its listeners no longer having all
their senses about them, the Nazi exploitation of
radio's 'resonating dimension' would consequently
be cited by media theorist Marshall McLuhan as a
prime example of the medium's "power to turn the
psyche and society into a single echo chamber".

Stockhausen remembered his mother's
relationship to the radio during the 1930s
in similar terms. "She would then talk to
the speaker on the radio", he recalled, "and
when she didn't get an answer she became very
furious. She couldn't understand that this was
a one-way box, a one-way message, and that she
had no chance to talk to this voice. I have
never forgotten that. I think she was right:
that the radio, from the start is an invention
which is incomplete, and if someone talks to
me, I should have a chance to talk back."

It's impossible to have a meaningful
dialogue with an echo, after all. Radio's very
invisibility had endowed it with the apparent
depth and power of music itself. Goebbels
consequently flew into a rage when an illustrated
weekly magazine published a photograph showing
the record of the fanfare used for the special
announcements that would interrupt regular
broadcasts during wartime. He insisted that the
musical illusion remain undisturbed at all costs,
even to the extent of threatening to punish any
further revelations of this kind with a stint in
the concentration camps. In the unseen, deeply
resonating dimension of radio, illusions work
best when they are allowed to interrupt the
normal flow of events. Broadcasting from New York
in 1938, Orson Welles caused mass panic with his
radio adaptation of *War of the Worlds* by having
news reports of a Martian invasion from outer
space interrupt a programme of light chamber
music. How well Goebbels would have understood
the cause of that collective terror. "It was
Hitler", McLuhan later affirmed, "who gave radio
the Orson Welles treatment for real."

Stockhausen's father was killed in combat
during the Second World War, while his mother,
institutionalised following a severe nervous
breakdown, was put to death by medical authorities
when the composer was just 13 years old.

●

Cut from individual rapture to collective
panic. Seen from the perspective of rubble
and mass graves, the virulent anti-Semitism
expressed in Richard Wagner's 1850 essay
"Judaism and Music" could no longer be
regarded as either a cultural contradiction
or the personal aberration of genius.
Such a response spoke at best of depraved
indifference. Wagner's music, Nietzsche
sarcastically remarked to those with ears to
hear him, represented a seductive combination
of "brutality, artificiality and innocence

(idiocy)". How would an enfeebled people ever survive without it?

In one of the newly occupied sectors of Berlin, a young Peter Thomas found work playing the piano in the Allied officers' clubs. "This was the first time as a German you could hear music from other countries", the composer would later recall of this post-war period. "Like a baby, I heard music of another kind." Most exciting of all were the big bands which Thomas encountered on British and American forces radio and in the 'Hit Kits' regularly supplied to the US sector. Thomas taught himself to perform a lot of this new material, formerly banned outright in Nazi Germany, so that he could use it in the clubs. "They'd ask for titles like 'Night and Day'. I didn't know what that was, but I had to play it the way the Americans wanted to hear it." At the same time sound engineers posted with RIAS (Radio in the American Sector) during the city's reconstruction discovered the Jesus Christus-Kirche in Berlin: a sublimely echoing space that registered well on the sensitive 'full frequency range' recording techniques developed during the Second World War. Pretty soon Deutsche Grammophon would be using the church's unique acoustic properties to bring an aura of sanctity to its classical music releases.

High-fidelity sound reproduction and higher frequency broadcasting meant that radio's resonating dimension was beginning to expand exponentially, its illusory power reaching further than ever before. The processes of recording and performing, receiving and transmitting would become radically transformed over the next two decades. As if to mark this intense period of transition, the gradual realisation of Karlheinz Stockhausen's *Kontakte* took place between early 1958 and the middle of 1960 in the electronic music studios at Westdeutscher Rundfunk, the German public broadcasting concern based in Cologne. Some of the equipment used for the piece contained parts from old US Army radio equipment; and the overall method for creating *Kontakte's* unique tones was similar to one developed in America by Bell Telephone Laboratories for synthesizing human speech. However, Stockhausen's audacious electronic score owes much of its range and scope to the composer's repositioning of the erase, record and playback heads on the WDR tape machines, allowing him to superimpose several layers of material at a time.

Such sounds could no longer be organised in conventional musical terms; the "air of another planet" had now been set in motion, shifting backwards and forwards across space between the left and right channels of a stereophonic speaker system, thanks to a Doppler effect Stockhausen achieves through the slowing down and speeding up of individual tones. Through the means of electronic realisation, music's invisibility is given a new plasticity, the points of 'contact' in *Kontakte* being conceived by the composer as those between the perceivable content of each electronically produced sound and its intangible effect. The results were subsequently released on record by Deutsche Grammophon.

As Stockhausen continued his experiments at WDR, the first Fluxus festivals of music took place in Northwest Germany. In 1961 George Maciunas, head of the Fluxus group in the US, had arrived in Germany to work as a civilian employee for the US Air Force. Soon joining him in evenings of 'action music' were the American poet Emmett Williams, employed by a military newspaper in Darmstadt at the time, the Berlin artist Wolf Vostell and Korean composer Nam Jun Paik, who was also exploring the new sound possibilities offered by the electronic music studio at WDR Cologne. A mixture of scripted performances, spontaneous provocations and simultaneous happenings, the Fluxus festivals were partially inspired by the ideas of the composer John Cage, who had increasingly come to regard the process of making music as a form of utopian social activity. The distinctions between form and content, performer and the audience, transcendence and the mundane became wilfully confused at events in which conventional instruments were systematically abused, household objects and electronic devices used to generate sounds, and the duration of individual pieces was dictated by chance or circumstance.

If nothing else, the Fluxus festivals of the early 1960s offered a brief moment of escape from music's unseen dimension, an evasion of its invisible power. In one playful gesture the perceivable had been wrenched from the intangible; but this separation was not to last. The two-day Festum-Fluxorum-Fluxus held in 1963 at the Düsseldorf Kunstakademie featured work by over 20 artists, including La Monte Young, Yoko Ono, Brion Gysin, Terry Riley and, for the first time, the Academy's

4 Karlheinz Stockhausen during the realisation of *Kontakte*, 1960. © Stockhausen Foundation for Music.

5 The Jesus Christus-Kirche in Dahlem, Berlin.

4

5

6

recently appointed professor of sculpture, Joseph Beuys.

Called up at age 19 in 1940, Beuys had first trained as an aircraft radio operator in the Luftwaffe; many of the Fluxus objects and performances he subsequently created in the 1960s involved the silent transmission or reproduction of sound. These include a number of 'silent' gramophones constructed from sausages, cushions, painted discs and animal bones, a grand piano completely encased in grey felt and a bone 'radio' tuned to 'an almost inaudible wavelength' in one of his most famous actions, *How to Explain Pictures to a Dead Hare*. Old, crudely fashioned and drably coloured, these makeshift pieces of audio equipment hinted at some unseen atavistic power: one that could not be accessed by conventional electronics.

Later dismissed by Maciunas as a form of Fluxus descended from "church procession, medieval fairs" and "Wagnerism" Beuys' work over this period was moving towards a restatement of the *gesamstkunstwerk* as something that radiated directly out of the artist's own presence. This was most plainly stated in the action *DER CHEF/ THE CHIEF (Fluxus Song)*, which Beuys staged in a Berlin gallery at the end of 1964. For eight

hours straight the artist lay on the floor, entirely wrapped in felt, making incoherent sounds into a microphone; a loudspeaker relayed the amplified sounds of breathing, coughing, sighing and mumbling, while a tape recorder played back a musical composition that had been created "in apparent contrast to Beuys' noises", according to Wolf Vostell, who witnessed the event. What intrigued Vostell most, however, was that the American artist Robert Morris was said to be carrying out exactly the same performance, synchronised to the second, at exactly the same time, "like an echo (the echo is a sculptural principle) in New York". Vostell's account makes an explicit connection between this synchronized 'echo' and Beuys' description of himself as a "transmitter", radiating outwards.

Ritualised and physical, requiring remarkable powers of endurance, *DER CHEF/THE CHIEF (Fluxus Song)* reaffirmed radio's status as a single echo chamber, even after Robert Morris revealed that he hadn't actually bothered to stage the corresponding action in New York. The transmitted Fluxus Song found its true response in another event that occurred across the Atlantic at the end of 1964. Using antennae at the Bell Telephone Laboratories in New Jersey

6 Nam Jun Paik's Prepared Piano during the exhibition Exposition of Music—Electronic Television, in Galerie Parnass, Wuppertal, Germany, 1963. © Nam June Paik Estate, Photo: Manfred Montwé

7 The Telstar communications satellite.

8 "Telstar" 7", Tornados.

and an outdated satellite transmission system appropriately named "Echo", American astronomer Robert Wilson and expatriate German physicist Arno Penzias detected a mysterious noise that was both present day and night and evenly distributed across the entire sky. This turned out to be low-level background radiation left over from the Big Bang: a cosmic echo of the massive explosion with which the universe had first begun.

●

Stars, radio static, music and the moral order had fallen into a new alignment by the end of 1964 as the West German Republic continued to reconstruct itself. In his influential political critique *One-Dimensional Man*, published that same year, the expatriate German philosopher Herbert Marcuse declared that "artistic alienation has become as functional as the architecture of the new theaters and concert halls in which it is performed". Works of art no longer posed a challenge to modern society, he argued; "the distance which made them *Luft von anderen Planeten* is conquered". The "air of another planet" seemed to have drawn a little closer since the dawn of the Space Age. What made the discovery of background radiation possible, after all, was the launch in 1962 of that pop-

culture bauble, the Telstar telecommunications satellite. As well as inspiring an otherworldly beat instrumental recorded by Joe Meek with the Tornados, Telstar had rendered the Echo satellite system obsolete, thereby freeing it up for Wilson and Penzias to use in their research. Orbiting the Earth, supplying Joe Meek and the Tornados with a massive international hit, Telstar linked outer space, electronic media, music and the future in a unique way. Thanks to the electrically amplified instruments, studio-generated echo and taped feedback featured on "Telstar", the *Luft von anderen Planeten* was emanating from every transistor radio in the West.

Popular culture and rapture had been on a collision course since 1908. The year in which Schoenberg incorporated Stephan George's poems into his *String Quartet No. 2* also marked the publication in the US of Hugo Gernsback's *Modern Electrics*, the world's first radio magazine. Gernsback quickly built up a successful publishing empire of magazines dedicated to popularizing science and technology, even going so far as to include some of the first ever pulp science-fiction tales. The Gernsback Publications logo was a modernist take on the Statue of Liberty's

8 Peter Thomas' soundtrack for Raumpatrouille, 1966.
9 Peter Thomas with his 12-oscillator synthesizer "Thomwiphon", 1968. Courtesy Peter Thomas.

torch transformed into a stylized radiant orb, discharging powerful beams of electricity.

Gernsback's early commercial success gave positive ideological expression to a notion of progress in which American industrial society emerged as the only true model for the future. The telecommunications satellite had transformed this future still further into something to be received: picked up by modern culture from another dimension. Having worked closely with Karlheinz Stockhausen at WDR and participated in Fluxus events alongside Joseph Beuys, Nam Jun Paik created *Moon is the Oldest TV*, the world's first video installation piece, in 1965. "What comes next?" Paik wrote in a letter to John Cage that same year. "In 1970 play moonlight sonata on the moon." However, as Marcuse observed in *One-Dimensional Man*, high culture belonged to an era before industrial civilisation. Electronic media in the 1960s now favoured the avant-garde to an unprecedented degree, bringing it further into the mainstream than ever before. There it had to share its visions of the future with TV shows like Raumpatrouille, an ambitious seven-part science-fiction co-production filmed in 1966 for broadcast in France and Germany. Set in the year 3000, the series recounts the fantastic adventures of the space ship Orion VIII patrolling the cosmos as "a small link in a security chain responsible for protecting the Earth from surprise attacks". Welcome to the paranoid utopia that is the West German Republic in the space age.

After writing scores for a large number of German-language cowboy adventures, FBI stories and Edgar Wallace mysteries, Peter Thomas had been commissioned to compose the title theme and incidental music for this new show. With no clear idea about what life would be like in outer space, Thomas modified the big band swing he learned to play in the Allied sectors of Berlin after Second World War for the *Raumpatrouille* soundtrack. Much of the futuristic shimmer and sparkle of these recordings was down to careful studio preparations in which the positioning of microphones played an important part in the musical arrangements. The brass section was given a cosmic edge by having female voices singing in unison delicately balanced against it; woodwinds were played back over distorting amplifiers to rough them up a little; and a Hammond organ was added to the mix, adding a modernist sheen to the harmonies. The countdown that introduced the show's opening theme was a precise echo of the one first used in Fritz Lang's *The Woman in the Moon* to build up tension in the film's dramatic launch sequence. Once a purely cinematic device, rocket scientists and space agencies have been using the same basic countdown ever since for pretty much the same effect. To add an extra dimension to the voice's impassive intoning of the numbers from *zehn* to *null*, Thomas ran it through a vocoder, giving each syllable a distinctly electronic tone.

Thanks to such studio trickery, the voyage outwards was more of a journey inwards than ever. With sound unable to travel in a vacuum, space had become the gap between stereo speakers: the sound of tomorrow transformed into a panned illusion moving from the left to the right channel. Predating the Apollo landings and the first modular synthesizers, Karlheinz Stockhausen's two-hour epic *Hymnen* electronically transformed the national anthems of the world into simulated shortwave signals, complete with call signs, crackling static and tuning transitions. "We are all transistors in the literal sense" Stockhausen affirmed in relation to *Hymnen*. "Waves arrive, antennae receive them, and the so-called high-fidelity system plays them back as directly as possible without distorting them too much." Realised on four-track tape at the WDR studios between 1966 and 1967, *Hymnen* presented the restless shifting of human consciousness as a type of radio frequency, alive with white noise, pure tonalities and cosmic radiation.

The future is not transmitted but received, even when the message is nothing but noise. "We can go one dimension deeper still" Stockhausen is heard announcing to a WDR engineer towards the middle of *Hymnen*, referring to the playback and overdubbing of material in that particular section. All wavelengths are forms of energy; all national identities become global ones. Being universal in nature, the starry heavens above and the moral law within can survive even changes of border. In an interview conducted in 1971 Stockhausen mentioned receiving a letter from a young German man who "completely went off and had a cosmic trip" after listening to shortwave signals over headphones for several hours, followed by the last two sections of *Hymnen*.

For it to have such an effect, the cosmos had to be transformed in the recording studio, pitched up or down electronically in order to fit within the human sensory spectrum. Its vastness was just another illusion, however. Humans only ever get to see or hear a humanized version of the universe: one that fits their waveband. The generation that had grown up after Second World War, raised exclusively on radio stations, pop music, movies and TV shows tended to take such limitations for granted. They all formed part of the electronic 'cosmic trip' and as such belonged neither to the utopian demands of the artistic avant-garde nor to the commercial constraints

of popular culture. If anything, the most distinctive music being produced in the West German Republic during the early 1970s appeared to have borrowed a little from both worlds. As awkward and absurd as the label foisted upon it, Krautrock was an amalgam of effects and influences.

Irmin Schmidt and Holger Czukay of Cologne-based outfit Can were students in Stockhausen's classes at Darmstadt during the mid-1960s, Czukay even using some of the composer's downtime at the WDR electronic music studios in 1968 to record *Canaxis*, his first solo project. At the same time Lothar Meid, bass player with the Munich collective Amon Düül II, was working in the studio with Peter Thomas, who was busily shaping Germany's future disco sound alongside electronics pioneer Giorgio Moroder. Czukay's use of lengthy tape loops to generate the two extended tracks that made up *Canaxis* and Meid's involvement in an ensemble that had developed out of a radical arts commune during the 1960s student movement have strong Fluxus overtones to them. The mistreating of conventional instruments to produce unconventional sounds, the embracing of technological means to create the music of tomorrow and an interest in pursuing a collective social agenda were all traits that Krautrock shared with Fluxus.

There is also something about the name for this new music, coming in off the airwaves as it does via late-night radio stations across Europe, which has some of the grim throwaway humour of early Fluxus about it. 'Kraut', after all, is a piece of slang tinged with wartime opprobrium and defeat; "rock" means "skirt" in German.

Such a casually ironic and modern term indicates an end to permanence echoed by a deep nostalgia for that permanence. The long drawn out tones, sustained decays and deep reverberations that have come to characterise Krautrock are all indications of a space that can no longer be filled—at least not by anything that lasts. The more cosmic and machine-like the music became, the less it could be related directly to the social politics of West Germany in the 1970s. Something similar can be detected in the manner Joseph Beuys presented himself as a transmitter not so much of a decipherable signal or discernable message but of energy itself, using electrical terminology to describe the artistic processes involved. "Terms like 'insulator', 'battery', 'transmitter', 'receiver' are all derived from the passage and storage

10 Stockhausen during the production of *Hymnen*, 1967.

© Stockhausen Foundation for Music.

of physical energy", Caroline Tisdall wrote
of his Fluxus objects in 1979, "but are drawn
into spiritual and anthropomorphic levels
by Beuys so that they become symbols and
metaphors of transformation and generate a
new concept of energy." The critic also went
on to describe how Beuys used "sound, noise,
melody using language" as sculptural materials.
Examined from the perspective of radio's unseen
dimension, the 'social sculpture' that Beuys
envisaged during the 1970s was yet another form
of *gesamstkunstwerk*, just like Syberberg's epic
film trilogy and Stockhausen's *Licht*, a cosmic
cycle of seven operas named after the days of
the week, both of which emanated from the same
troubled decade.

West Germany's deeper dimension was also
an emptier one. "We were nowhere" Kraftwerk's
Ralf Hütter revealed to the *NME* in 1981, just
as Syberberg's movie adaptation of Wagner's
Parsifal went into production. Time had turned
into space again. "You more and more doubt
what's happening and where you stand", Hütter
commented of his experiences growing up in the
British sector and the Westdeutscher Rundfunk
catchment area. "It has nothing to do with
nationalistic feelings, it's more a cultural
thing—it has to do with more spiritual feelings,
continental feelings…"

In 1975 Kraftwerk 'gave radio the Orson
Welles treatment' by restaging *War of the*
Worlds as a series of interruptions on their
Radio-Aktivität album; disembodied voices
break through the music, claiming to speak
on behalf of the stars, radio waves, uranium
isotopes and, perhaps least surprising of
all, Westdeutscher Rundfunk. After a brief
intermission made up of station call signs
on "Sendepause" a WDR announcer can be heard
leading off "Nachrichten": a montage of muffled
and deadened radio news reports on the continuing
proliferation of nuclear power stations in
the West German Republic. Starting with the
crackling of radio static, the clicking of
Geiger counters and abrupt bursts of Morse
code, *Radio-Aktivität* is a carefully sustained
examination of a past that remains "in the air
for you and me", according to the ethereal
title track. Even the album's front cover,
created by Emil Schult (a former student of
Joseph Beuys' at the Düsseldorf Kunstakademie),
makes prominent display of the Deutscher
Kleinempfänger radio receiver, first manufactured
in 1938 and quickly known among the German
listening public as "Goebbels' snout". Even the
once forbidden shortwave band makes a pointed
appearance on the song "Radioland", where it
is celebrated as a source of electronic tones
strikingly similar to the ones Stockhausen had
produced at WDR while working on *Kontakte*,
right down to the Doppler effect between the
recording's left and right channels.

Imagine you are standing alone on a craggy windswept sea cliff beneath a moonless night sky. You spread your arms out at your side like superhero wings and you slowly begin to ascend, a dreamlike absorption into the dark embrace of the galaxy. Your pace quickens until you are rocketing through the stars like a spectral eyeball shot out of a quantum canon. The immensity of space swallows you up, and as nearly all of the perceptual frameworks you normally use to process reality evaporate, you become profoundly and ecstatically disoriented. Boundaries melt, nowhere is up or down, and your immense speed has morphed into a glacial drift. Your tiny mind is blown as you attempt to compass the conundrum of the infinite, and to plumb the meaning of the flickering flash of awareness you call your life in light of this vast void of shifting three-dimensional geometries, this empty and shattered immensity, this *cosmos*.

released on Rolf-Ulrich Kaiser's Kosmische Musik label. Kosmische musik, in my mind, seems to be a crucial strand of the progressive psychedelic music that appeared in Germany in the early 1970s: an alternately meditative and ferocious dissolution of boundaries that invoked, through sound or function or packaging, the unearthly otherworlds that link outer and inner space.

But this only begs the question: what does it mean to speak of the cosmic in music?

To edge toward an answer, we must first strip the word of its purely scientific or positivist connotations. The cosmic is never just the brute fact of the material universe, but the cluster of feelings, imaginings, and spiritual intuitions that arise when we try to wrap our minds and hearts around that immense fact—or to make art from such inevitably fragile wrappings.

KOSMISC

Erik Davis

Now here's the question: what soundtrack was playing during your trip?

If you heard hard-ass hippie freak-out rock replete with bongos, scattershot guitar solos, and feedbacking flutes, or if you heard spectral and atonal Moogified soundscapes too rock'n'roll to count as avant-garde music and too experimental to count as rock'n'roll—in other words, if you heard Krautrock—then you are not quite as alone as you might have felt when you first turned to face the universe. You are, at the very least, standing there with Edgar Froese, who first used the term kosmische musik to characterise the music Tangerine Dream started to make with their deep space electronics-heavy second album, 1971's *Alpha Centauri*. Though kosmische musik is sometimes conflated with the general category of Krautrock, my ears tell me that some crucial Krautrock bands—Can and NEU!—are not nearly as kosmische as acts like Tangerine Dream, Klaus Schulze, Popol Vuh, and a lot of the records

The cosmic, in other words, is not just an object but a quality of consciousness.

What sort of quality?

For the ancient Greeks, *kosmos* meant an "orderly arrangement"; in Homer, *kosmeo* describes the practice of marshalling troops. The ancient geometry shaman Pythagoras, who believed that number and mathematical form lay at the heart of reality, was probably the first thinker to use *kosmos* to characterise the material universe, which, as you might expect, was imagined to be an ordered and harmonious whole. Pythagoras' famous concept of the "music of the spheres", which is hardly unrelated in spirit to kosmische musik, derived from his belief that the mathematical ratios that underlie harmonic musical overtones are also incarnated in the structure of the heavens—particularly the ratios of planetary orbits, which were imagined as onion-skin like spheres nested within one another. By the time of Plato,

(C) Sternenmädchen Media Service GmbH

1

HE

1 Back card design from the *Sternenmädchen's Tarot*. Conceived by Rolf-Ulrich Kaiser and Gille Lettmann, illustrated by Peter Geitner, 1975. Courtesy tarotgarden.com.

2 (overleaf) Holger Trülzsch and Florian Fricke of Popol Vuh, in the Italian magazine Ciao2001, 1973. Courtesy Dolf Mulder.

kosmos had come to denote the entire visible universe, a balanced and ordered whole that was crafted by a wise demiurge who made his creation beautiful as well as true. This element of beauty is key to the classic philosophical account. In the *Timaeus*, Plato describes the cosmos not only as the holistic incarnation of rational and geometric principles, but also as a kind of living creature, "the fairest and most perfect of intelligible beings".

When we gaze up at the night sky, or when we analyze the sacred geometry seemingly carved into the planetary orbits or our astrological natal charts, we can still sniff the atmosphere of beauty and perfection that inspired the old Greeks and their craftsman cosmos. The contemporary fact that the universe displays self-similar structures on the greatest of scales—patterns born just microseconds after the Big Band that still striate the whole enchilada—is enough to give anyone a Platonic flashback. But another quality has entered our experience of the cosmos as well: a stern and sometimes self-immolating feeling of immensity

Pop tedesco

COSMISCHE MUSIK

MUSICA COSMICA, SPAZI VERGINI E INFORMALI
CON TANGERINE DREAM; MEDITAZIONE ELETTRONICA CON ATMOSFERE
ROMANTICO-ORIENTALI NEI POPOL VUH (NELLA FOTO),
ASH RA TEMPEL; PREISTORIA
E FUTURISMO CON I KRAFTWERK; CAMPUS MUSIC, NOTE POLITICHE
IN EMBRYO E FLOH DE COLOGNE.

and awe mixed with disorientation, loneliness, even fear. The cosmos, it seems, is no more beautiful than it is inhospitable. Cataclysmic explosions abound; meteorites have pulverised planet earth (and will do so again); and the inconceivable number of galaxies itself undermines whatever comfort we might take in cosmic existence with the sheer absurdity of the situation. Outside of faith communities, few of us can even imagine the old idea of a master creator: Pythagoras' composer or Plato's craftsman or the good Lord who rules it all. The awe we feel confronted by a desert night-sky, the awe that lays at the hot heart of the kosmische, is, in a sense, the after-image of this now absent demiurge.

This ghost of God has replaced the mantle of the sacred with the more modern condition of the *sublime*—a concept and aesthetic experience that remains one of the major cultural sources of the kosmische vibe. Though most associated with the blasted heaths and crashing waves of Romanticism, the notion of the sublime arose roughly a century earlier, at the onset of the Age of Enlightenment, when well-heeled British tourists on the road to Italy got freaked out by the Alps. Making their way through the mountains, gentlemen like Joseph Addison and the third Earl of Shaftesbury glimpsed a craggy and ruinous landscape whose jagged expanse powerfully moved their souls in a pleasurable if disturbing manner that had little to do with the well-proportioned sense of beauty that the ancients associated with the craftsman's cosmos. Addison's account of his 1699 tour is peppered with terms like "unbounded" and "unlimited"—terms of excess and boundary dissolution rather than proportion and harmony. This dissolution of borders, coupled with a sense of immensity and expressive chaos, became hallmarks of the sublime.

Inevitably the philosophers sunk their teeth into this spooky but cognitive thrill, a specifically modern feeling that was also a new way of seeing the world, and especially the world of nature. In the middle of the eighteenth century, Edmund Burke boldly contrasted the sublime with the beautiful, characterising the aesthetic pleasure of the former as a sense of astonishment mixed with fear, a heady brew that could be evoked by objects marked by "vastness, infinity, magnificence". A few decades later, Immanuel Kant took up the baton in his *Critique of Judgment*. Laying the groundwork for the *mise-en-scène* of a thousand horror films and gothic novels to come, Kant wrote that nature stirs up the idea of the sublime "in its chaos, or in its wildest and most irregular disorder and desolation, provided it gives signs of magnitude and power". Kant contrasted the bounded limits of the beautiful object with the boundlessness of the sublime environment. But the philosopher suggested something even more trippy: that the feeling of sublimity does not really lie in the object at all, however dizzying and immense. Instead, that rush of unnerving awe lies precisely in the *failure* of the human imagination to fully grasp the thing it confronts. In other words, the sublime lies within, a swirling void that expands just beyond that cliff edge where we reach the limits of our own vision, even—though Kant himself would not say this—the limits of our own reason.

Stand with me and Froese at the edge of this cliff, and you will see how the rhetoric of the sublime infected the modern experience of the kosmische. From the moment that Galileo peered through his amplified glass and bespyed the rings of Saturn, telescopes and their spectrum-scanning descendents have produced a picture of the universe that is constantly expanding in both its details and its magnitude (not to mention its startling paradoxes). You can get a glimmer of the giddiness this perpetual perceptual expansion can induce by recalling that, only a century ago, the majority of astronomers still believed the universe contained only a single galaxy. The limits of the Milky Way were the limits of the cosmos. Then Edwin Hubble started analyzing images captured with Mount Wilson's 100-inch telescope in Southern California. Realising that the variable stars nestled in some distant spiral nebulae lay far beyond boundaries of the Milky Way, he concluded that these nebulae were galaxies like our own, a few of what we now know are hundreds of billions of star clumps. Moreover, by comparing the red shift of these distant stellar objects, Hubble also grokked that the universe was constantly expanding—a giddy and somewhat nauseating prospect that literally exploded whatever static assumptions remained from the clockwork universe of the ancients.

Hubble's expansion of the physical universe through both space and time is a perfect expression of the sublime object that dissolves boundaries and overwhelms our imagination (what Kant would call the mathematical sublime). Indeed, it is in the cosmos that the sublime finds its final, perhaps terminal home. The raging

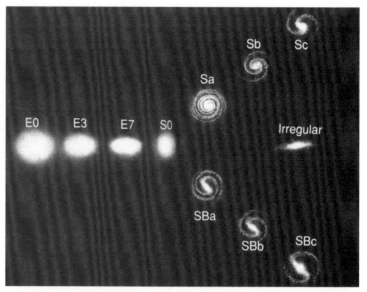

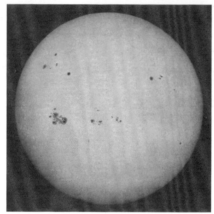

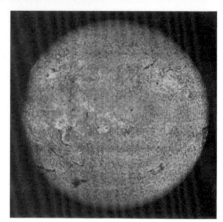

3

storms and craggy moors of the Romantic era, when the sublime became a crucial aesthetic category, have now been leached of their intensity through over-expose and cliché. We've all seen that movie. Driving along the highways of the Alps today, we think of postcards and Disneyland rides. But when we pour over tarted-up photos of nebulae from the Hubble telescope, or simply follow the current astronomical picture, with all its paradoxes, gaps, and immensities, we can still taste an unironic and sometimes startling sense of the sublime—"an emotion", wrote Kant, "that seems to be no sport, but dead earnest in the affairs of the imagination".

Though rooted in the confrontation with nature's extremes, the sublime is an essentially aesthetic quality, and so inevitably became woven into western art, and especially into the abstract and somewhat boundless art of music. From Beethoven to Bruckner to Strauss,

the Romantic symphonic music grappled with vast imponderables. After a century of atonality, noise, and chthonic electric guitars, most of this music seems pretty tame to our ears, far too measured and melodically restrained to conjure the alien and "dead earnest" quality of the cosmic—that quality that HP Lovecraft would have called *outsideness*. Holst's famous suite *The Planets*, written during the First World War, is the last gasp of a charming clockwork solar system that would soon be pulverised by quantum mechanics and, on the musical front, serialism. These twin shocks made many early twentieth-century composers wary of the cosmic and its overheated rhetoric of the sublime.

But one can never fully repress the cosmos— that picture of the universe that we can never do without, and that, whatever its degree of materialism, continues to incarnate mystery. In the post-war world, the cosmic slipped back into

4

3 Clockwise from top left: Edwin Hubble with the Mount Wilson
telescope. Edwin Hubble's classification of galaxies.
Photographs of the sun taken at the Mount Wilson Observatory.
4 The cover of Tangerine Dream's *Zeit*, 1972.

music. Olivier Messiaen's immense imaginative
investment in a creative but God-centered universe
gave a lot of his brash and colorful large-scale
symphonic work an undeniable galactic dimension.
By the late 1950s, Messiaen's student Stockhausen
was paring his serial and electronic experiments
with a cosmic sensibility that was both mystical
and mathematical. Stockhausen, a longhair who
would later meditate before his performances like
a good Krautrocker, described the shift in post-
war music as "an orientation away from mankind…
Once again one looked up to the stars and began
an intensive measuring and counting."

It is a more than a kosmische coincidence
that Stockhausen's musical mysticism manifested
itself partly through electronics. As listeners
of Klaus Schulze, Tangerine Dream, and Popol
Vuh recognise, the timbre and tonality of
electronic instruments are fundamental to the
kosmische vibe. Why? In the nineteenth century,

the technological capture of electricity and
electro-magnetic effects went hand-in-hand with
the conceptual revolution introduced by the
recognition of the electromagnetic spectrum, a
literally universal field of invisible vibrating
reality that, inevitably, created a scientific
if no longer strictly materialist basis for
the occult consciousness of higher spiritual
dimensions. The fundamentally cosmic dimension
of electronic sound notably asserts itself in
the peculiar fate of the theremin, one of the
first electronic instruments, and certainly—with
its spectral tone and incorporeal interface—one
of the spookiest. Though Clara Rockmore used the
instrument to perform the classics at Carnegie
Hall, the device had performed a classic high-
brow/low-brow flip-flop by the 1950s, when film
composers started milking the thing for eerie
and often extraterrestrial exotica in the
soundtracks for flicks like *Spellbound, The Day*

5

the Earth Stood Still, and The Thing. Cosmic sounds can be sublime, even alienating, but they are also pop.

Perhaps the most resonant instance of such a galactic crossover between experimentalism and the popcorn crowd occurred when Stanley Kubrick appropriated a couple pieces by the Hungarian composer György Ligeti in the 1960s. In his mountainous chromatic choral works Lux Aeterna and Requiem, Ligeti layered fluctuating lines and hair-splitting intervals according to invisible rules of "micropolyphany". (As with much of Stockhausen's work, Ligeti's music was much less "chaotic" than it sounded on its surface.) With its constantly drifting harmonic vectors, the music sounded as if it were trying to orient itself in deep space by drifting in all directions at once. Without permission, Kubrick sampled these works for the soundtrack to 2001: A Space Odyssey. The Requiem's eerie "Kyrie" was unforgettably pared with the appearance of the extraterrestrial monolith that heralds and may actually trigger breakthroughs in human consciousness—breakthroughs that, in the experimental trip sequence that closes the film anyway, take place through an arduous visionary passage through the sublime.

The strange fate of Ligeti's choral works—a fate that fuses religion, science fiction, avant-garde music, and pop psychedelia—sets the stage for the proper emergence of German kosmische musik. If we rightly refuse to use the term kosmische to tag the whole progressive psychedelic German music scene, we can reserve it for a musical sensibility that fluctuates between two largely improvisatory poles of interstellar overdrive. On the one hand, you find yourself sucked towards the black holes that lie at the heart of the heaviest jams laid down by Amon Düül II and Ash Ra Tempel: a ferociously intense psychedelic spooge-fest whose disavowal of the usual Anglo-American blues substratum signals a formal transcendence of the planet and its "earthy" music. At the other pole, the kosmische freespace loses all structural relationship to rock'n'roll, even to rhythm and tonality, and becomes the literally groundbreaking "space music" of early Tangerine Dream and Irrlicht-era Klaus Schulze.

What unites the poles of this sacred dyad of interstellar freakery is the quality of boundlessness. The heavy psychedelic jams grow stronger the more they can incarnate the sublime freak philosophy of "anything goes", while the proto-ambient soundscapes of Tangerine Dream and others erode traditional melodic, harmonic, and rhythmic markers. These two musical strategies—often combined, as in the better Cosmic Jokers recordings—also reflect what Arthur Schopenhauer characterised, in The World as Will and Representation, as the "twofold nature" of sublime consciousness. When confronted with convulsive and immense eruptions of nature, Schopenhauer argued, we feel in touch with forces that can annihilate us; we are "helpless against powerful nature, dependent, abandoned to chance, a vanishing nothing in the face of stupendous forces." On the other hand, Schopenhauer describes the deeper peace that arises on a deeper level than such struggle, as the subject—or listener—"feels himself as the eternal, serene subject of knowing, who as the condition of every object is the supporter of this whole world."

6

In the sublime dialectic of the kosmische, titanic and inhuman struggles are mysteriously pared with a serene acceptance of an underlying unity. This deeply psychedelic logic produces the peculiar fusion of drive and drift that characterises the more mystical dimensions of Krautrock. After all, since few longhaired German musicians were serving as astronauts or even astronomers in the early 1970s, the sublime cosmos they were mapping with their music was one they discovered inside their own awareness—what the Canadian psychiatrist Richard Bucke was probably the first to call, in his famous 1901 book, "cosmic consciousness". Remember: the kosmische is always a quality of the mind as well as an object. Popol Vuh's "Vuh", from *In Den Gärten Pharaos*, is utterly cosmic, and yet it seems to radiate from within an ancient crypt rather than a black hole at the heart of a distant galaxy. The sublime is a mode of spirit; in the end, it needs no science-fiction prop to justify its wacked-out plunge into the resplendent void. Just don't look before you leap.

IM GLÜCK

Michel Faber

The first person who ever played me any German rock music was a German. Reinhardt was the older brother of a schoolfriend and, despite the huge age difference between us (I was 16, he was pushing 20), he loaned me his reel-to-reel tape machine and a stack of tapes. Looking back, I can't imagine why he took this risk, other than that he was keen to share some of the stuff he liked, stuff that evidently meant to him what Deep Purple and Status Quo meant to the Anglo kids at my school. The debut album by NEU! was on those reels. So was *Sturmvogel*, an LP by East German band Puhdys. I presume you know NEU!; that's why you're reading this book. You may never have heard of Puhdys. In the 33 years since I borrowed Reinhardt's tapes, I've never seen Puhdys mentioned by the kinds of journalists and musicians for whom NEU! are gods. Yet, in Germany, despite being hampered by the GDR's restrictions on capitalist enterprise, Puhdys attained a level of success our gods could never reach. Clad in truly eye-molesting outfits (think Mud or Showaddywaddy) and purveying an odd mixture of singalong ballads, prog and 1950s-style rock'n'roll, Puhdys went from strength to strength, eventually celebrating their thirtieth anniversary by selling out the 23,000-seat Waldbühne in post-unification Berlin.[1] Last time I saw Faust, even with the benefit of three decades of reverence from English journalists, they played to a hundredth of that number in a club in Elephant & Castle.

This discrepancy shouldn't surprise us. We know that avant-garde music is not stadium fare. We know that The Velvet Underground played to poky beer dives while The Rolling Stones held court at Madison Square Gardens. We know that right now, in 2009, we can check out the latest dubstep pioneer in the company of 30 likeminded souls while, elsewhere in town, Bon Jovi will be defying all laws of terminal redundancy by basking in the applause of multitudes. What allows us to make sense of these scenarios is that we're familiar with The Rolling Stones and Bon Jovi, familiar with the mass tastes that support them, familiar with the landscapes of English and American rock generally. We know where avant-garde music fits in the picture. But when it comes to Krautrock, in the absence of any wider picture of the German rock landscape, we are in danger of mythologising Germany as a

incl. 33min. version of solar-music

BRAIN
metronome
2/1050
STEREO

ballermann

2

1 Grobschnitt from *Solar Music Live*, 1978.

2 Grobschnitt *Ballermann*, 1974.

place where cool proto-electronica once reigned supreme and where veteran Krautrock innovators nowadays enjoy the sort of "lifetime achievement" status accorded to David Bowie or Frank Zappa.

Sadly, no. Let me give it to you straight: the krauts aren't into Krautrock. Leaving aside unease about the term itself (yes, I know it's tongue-in-cheek, but imagine defending the humour of "Chink-rock" or "Wop-rock" to a Chinese or an Italian) Germans are not that interested in the bands we think are so sublime. I've talked to a lot of Germans over the years, quizzing them about their musical tastes. And you know what I've discovered? Germans like jazz. They like blues. They like heavy rock. They adore Bob Dylan. The younger ones like techno. Or heavy metal. The older ones have a soft spot for some British prog-rock groups who were second-

MICHEL FABER

3 Grobschnitt *Ballermann* inner artwork, 1974.

stringers in Britain but who ruled the roost in
Europe (eg, Manfred Mann's Earthband). And they
love Bob Dylan (or did I already mention that?)
They want to know if you've heard the mindblowing
bootleg of Dylan at Alsterdorfer Sporthalle in
April 2002 where he does a completely different
version of "Desolation Row".

I once befriended a German musician who
played bass in a covers band in the north of
Scotland. His happiest memories were of his
stint in a reggae combo back in Düsseldorf.
The motorik beat of Klaus Dinger was alien to
him; he could debate the finer points of jazz
technique, eloquently describe the patter
of Roy Haynes's brushes on a ride cymbal. He
had an impeccable collection of Blue Note
and ECM albums. If nudged into nostalgia for
his misspent youth, he revealed an enduring
fondness for Australian pub-rockers Cold Chisel.
Obviously he'd heard Kraftwerk, but then,
hasn't everybody? Of the other German bands I
mentioned, most had passed him by, or had been
rejected as unworthy of investigation. The only
one he seemed familiar with—indeed, he'd seen
them play in his home town—was Grobschnitt.

Grobschnitt were the archetypal German
rock band: a hard-gigging bunch of loony
extroverts who would co-opt any style of music
if it raised a cheer from the crowd. Spinal
Tap is a fair comparison, but so is Zappa's
Mothers Of Invention. Concerts were wild three-

hour parties characterised by madcap skits,
pyrotechnics, psychedelic guitar freakouts,
prog pomp, satirical theatre, and—always—crack
musicianship. Their signature piece "Solar
Music"—first released as a 33-minute studio
version on 1974's *Ballermann* and stretched out
in endless live permutations afterwards—is no
less ambitious than, say, "Apocalypse In 9/8" by
Genesis or "A Plague Of Lighthouse Keepers" by
Van der Graaf Generator, but there's something
hermetically private, even neurotic, about those
English pieces, whereas in Grobschnitt's hands,
the same sort of material is whipped up into a
communal celebration of Dionysiac exuberance.

Come to grips with Grobschnitt and you're
half-way to understanding what the 1970s were
really like for the vast numbers of intelligent
German rock fans who didn't bother to turn up
at NEU! gigs.

NEU! did play live, you know—for a while.
Audiences were small and often left dissatisfied.
Reviews were few and could be harsh. Discouraged
and broke, the band stopped playing in public.
As for Michael Rother's next project, the
'supergroup' Harmonia, they were hardly a
supergroup in the Crosby, Stills, Nash &
Young sense: Rother calls them a "commercial
disaster", and remembers that "in 1974 we once
played to an audience of three people. I can
laugh now but it wasn't funny back then. Most
people in Germany hated our music." This is

confirmed by Rudi Vogel, manager of a Krautrock mail order company and compiler of the five-CD box set *Krautrock: Music For Your Brain*. He told me: "Even in the music magazines, Krautrock was almost totally ignored. The German [critics] preferred American West Coast, Bob Dylan, Neil Young, Grateful Dead and stuff like that." In 1972, Tangerine Dream were literally bottled off the stage at Bayreuth by bored Bavarians wanting a blues band. The prickly, pompous self-belief displayed nowadays by Edgar Froese and Klaus Schulze is not mere egomania: in the 1970s, in their own country, these men truly were prophets without honour.

Our conviction that Krautrock is 'timeless' and has therefore never become 'dated' is one that few Germans share. We perceive the genre in simplified terms, a few iconic bands in a pristine vacuum. Most Germans see those same bands as part of an ocean of bygone naffness, a clownish horde of hirsute hippies in preposterous clothes. Nobody in Britain or the USA, when picturing Can or Ash Ra Tempel, is afflicted by associated images of Eloy or Jane or Curly Curve indulging in gross guitar wankery. Our ignorance of the musical world beyond English-language journalism may be regrettable, but we use it as a filter. It means we can remain blissfully unaware of the German equivalents of, say, Supertramp, REO Speedwagon, Heart, Foreigner, Peter Frampton, Ted Nugent, Lynyrd Skynyrd, Dr Hook, Foghat, Kiss, Kansas and on and on ad infinitum.

Distaste provoked by a musical past can lead to an elective amnesia, a denial of a once-shared reality. I mentioned to Rudi Vogel my puzzlement at how many Germans I'd met did not seem to have noticed much Krautrock at all, despite being the right age to have witnessed it unfolding. He replied, with weary sardonicism: "Your remark about all the Germans who do not know Krautrock is interesting. Most of the folks with whom I spent my youth do not know the term 'Krautrock', in spite of having spent many days at the concerts and listened to many of the famous LPs." Of course, something similar happens in our own culture, when we meet people who talk about having grown up with The Sex Pistols or Public Enemy rather than admitting that the first album they bought was Fleetwood Mac's Rumours, or that they used to stare at their older brother's copy of Barclay James Harvest's *Octoberon* hoping for a flash of mystical enlightenment. The past is a different country and many people have difficulty remembering that they ever lived there.

Even those Germans who are up for a bit of Krautrock have a handicap: they cannot perceive 1970s German music as a phenomenon that burned brightly and then disappeared. That's how we see it, because we've chosen to venerate bands who bowed out before their mystique could be eroded by punk, MTV and advancing age. Eruption and Xhol Caravan vanished as early as 1972, Ash Ra Tempel went their separate ways in 1973, Agitation Free, Brainticket, Faust, NEU! and Harmonia quit mid-decade, Cluster and Can dissolved in 1979, Amon Düül II admitted defeat two years later. Even Kraftwerk—in theory the most long-lived of the seminal krautrock groups—have produced only two albums of new material since 1981, preferring to maintain their legendary status with concerts and remixes of their 1970s recordings.[2]

Diminishing returns for the listener? Not necessarily. Our hunger for fresh 1970's sounds is regularly satisfied by archaeological discoveries of ever-more-obscure groups—Dom, Emtidi, Bröselmaschine, Ainigma, Kalacakra, etc—who, unheard of since their moment in the sun, seem to exist in a temporal Shangri-La, preserved as beautiful young maidens and intense young men for ever. The German public, however, don't look through that end of the telescope. To them, German rock is a messy story of countless bands exceeding their sell-by date, a saga of ageing showbiz stalwarts struggling to adapt to changing fashions.

Broadly speaking, the same factors were at play in Germany as anywhere else in the western world. Disco, punk, New Wave ("Neue Deutsche Welle"), the rise of corporate rock, rap, computerised recording techniques and click tracks, world music, the unplugged phenomenon, and so on. Studying the cream of Krautrock doesn't help us much to understand how these trends affected Germany, because we chose that cream precisely for its lack of contamination. But even within our hallowed "canon", there are a few clues. You just have to be open-minded enough to perceive some of your heroes' late-1970s albums as fresh departures rather than dying gasps.

Klaus Dinger's La Düsseldorf fused punk, disco, electronica and a bizarre shimmer of Eurovision kitsch into a winning formula. Their

KALACAKRA

CRAWLING TO LHASA

4

4 Kalacakra *Crawling to Lhasa*, 1972. Courtesy Garden of Delights.
5 Ainigma *Diluvium*, 1973. Courtesy Garden of Delights.
6 Emtidi S/T, 1970. Courtesy Garden of Delights.

5

1978 album *Viva* was a big success in Germany, but its impact in Britain was hampered by xenophobic radio playlists and the collapse of Radar, the band's UK record company. (Had they been signed to Virgin, who knows how they'd have fared? We don't like to admit it, but sometimes, it's licensing and distribution deals that determine which 'foreign' acts we recognise as artistically important.) *Viva* triumphantly bridged the gap between 'classic' Krautrock and the 1980s. By contrast, Klaus Dinger's 1985 solo effort *Néondian* (*La Düsseldorf 4*), was hampered by the clinical production, pre-fab keyboard sounds and gated pseudo-drums that were imposed on many other albums from the same era.

Amon Düül II were dedicated, from inception, to reflecting the changing times. By the mid-1970s, expecting to find them playing *Yeti*-style psychedelic freakouts was like expecting David Bowie to still be a long-haired hippy performing "The Wild-Eyed Boy From Freecloud". Partly driven by their desire to remain 'relevant' and partly lured by the carrot of American success, the band drafted in younger players and kept gigging. Krautrock purists choke on albums like *Only Human* and *Almost Alive*, fine though these are on their own terms. Typically, the German press approved of the band's evolution away from the lysergic peripheries. "Amon Düül

II aus Revoluzzern wurden absolute Profis"[3], declared the *Abendzeitung* newspaper, meaning it as praise. By the end of the decade, however, the band itself had grown uneasy with its pop flirtations and reunited its classic lineup to make the uncompromisingly weird (if somewhat coldly produced) *Vortex*, an album that failed to find an audience in 1980s Germany.

It's in the careers of more populist and/or longer-lived bands that the march of the zeitgeist can be most clearly observed. Grobschnitt may have elicited cheers from their 1979 audiences when they defiantly shouted "Eine tote Village People ist eine gute Village People!"[4] before ripping into the disco parody "A.C.Y.M", but they soon found themselves under increasing pressure from a modish marketplace. Their 1982 album *Razzia* (sleeved in a design that wouldn't have been out of place on a Toto or Ultravox LP) showed the influence of the contemporary crop of poodle-haired heavy metal bands, as well as some new wave touches and a plaintive pop single "Wir Wollen Leben".[5] As though personally doubtful of this message, founder member Eroc then left the band, and Grobschnitt's subsequent efforts were disfigured by Simmons drums, blaring synth-brass and bland MOR.

6

Guru Guru started off as the ultimate lysergic power trio, playing agitprop concerts for the Socialist German Student Union, living in a bus on a diet of LSD. As times changed, they graduated to Mahavishnu-style jazz fusion ("Hope you like our new direction," as Spinal Tap might say) before incorporating mainstream rock, Latin grooves, lame pop, easy listening, rap, Goa tribalism and trance.[6]

Kraan, who had spent the 1970s perfecting their distinctive brand of eastern-inflected jazz-funk, likewise found their freewheeling aesthetic difficult to maintain. Songs shrank to radio length, improvs were curtailed. By 1982 they were without a record deal, returning only in 1989, short-haired and smart-jacketed, with *Dancing In The Shade*, which showed a strong influence of The Police, U2 and Comsat Angels.[7] Similar compromises were forced upon formerly million-selling stadium rock bands like Jane and Birth Control, whose 1980s output was as

7 Eroc in 1983. Courtesy Eroc.

unfortunate as anything produced in those same years by Starship or Rainbow. Indeed, the same story was played out in the careers of hundreds of bands, major and minor. While it would be unfair to allege that all the old hippies cut their hair short, donned Miami Vice clothes and bought Yamaha DX7 synths, it also needs saying that, exactly as in the UK and US, the German music industry was no longer prepared to fund the left-wing utopian experimentalism of anarchic flower children.

In our own culture, we've often observed worthy musicians losing their way during the 1980s, getting back on track in the mid-1990s and, after the hurdle of the new millennium, producing superb material once more. This pattern is evident in Germany, too. But we are also familiar with artists whose sellouts during the Thatcher and Reagan years were not reversible, artists who are tainted by corporate sponsorship deals, crass exploitation of their fans, and artistic bankruptcy. Just so in Germany. And this is another reason why Krautrock is held in less esteem over there than elsewhere. Too many bands (almost none of whom figure in our highly selective pantheon) are still soldiering on, getting wrinklier and balder and fatter, producing increasingly dreadful albums, going on TV chat shows to talk about divorce and rehab, exhorting their audiences to sing along like it's "yesterday once more". For a young German who wants to be cool, the temptation to toss these old farts in the dustbin of history—along with the whole 1970s gene pool that spawned them—must be very strong indeed.

In conclusion, don't get me wrong: I'm not arguing that Krautrock deserves less reverence than we give it. Its best artists are still awe-inspiring and its best albums are still miraculous. The Germans are wrong to kneel before Bob Dylan, Neil Young and all the other mainstays of *Mojo* and *Rolling Stone*, if such subjugation by an Anglocentric narrative of rock history blinds them to the greatness that their own country has produced. Nor am I saying that Krautrock, when seen in its entirety rather than in our carefully filtered selection, bears out the old maxim that 99.99 per cent of everything is crap. To my ears, even a run-of-the-mill German album from the 1970's has more charm than a run-of-the-mill British or American one. 1970s Germany *was* special.

But we must understand that Germany did not call an end to history when NEU!, Can, Sergius

Golowin and sundry other cosmic couriers vanished from the scene. Life went on. Shops got restocked, restocked again, then went bust and got replaced by other shops. People grew older and had kids and those kids are now grown up too. My own experience of growing up, thanks to Reinhardt and a few other *displaced* Germans, gave me Krautrock—not too much of it, nor too little, just enough of it to thoroughly enchant me. No matter what I learn about the genre subsequently, nothing can harm the innocent purity of the original love affair. So, the next time I meet a German who couldn't give a toss about Harmonia's *Deluxe* but wants to tell me about Keith Jarrett or AC-DC or the magnificent performance of "Blowin' In The Wind" that Bob did in Bologna, I shouldn't feel bemused. I should feel… *im Glück*.[8]

1. Puhdys are still very much in business, reinventing themselves with every new musical trend, and racking up revised Greatest Hits packages as more decades pass. They recently duetted with Rammstein.

2. Some of these groups got back together in the 1980s and 1990s, but the Krautrock narrative favoured by journalists almost invariably ignores such reunions. Thus, veteran musicians who regard themselves as alive and active are regarded by the press as dead and gone, and the myth of a self-contained 1970s is maintained.

To be honest, however, not many of the seminal 1970s Krautrock acts have been able to reconnect vigorously with their muse. Faust is a notable exception. After a hiatus of almost twenty years, they resumed making thrilling, exploratory music without pandering to nostalgia. The noise they make has some kinship with industrial bands like Einstürzende Neubauten, but remains wonderfully unpredictable.

The post-1970s work of Ash Ra Tempel mainman Manuel Göttsching and Cluster composer Hans-Joachim Roedelius has also argued a continuity between classic Krautrock and later music trends (in this case, trance and new age). The results have varied from lovely to innocuous. New age and trance were also the vehicles of choice for Popol Vuh, a group who had won a high profile in the 1970s for their work with film director Werner Herzog but who (despite one last soundtrack in the 1980s) faded from the scene as leader Florian Fricke turned to playing Mozart and pursuing an alternative career as a music therapist. However, the final album before Fricke's death, *Messa Di Orfeo*, was a pleasingly peculiar return to experimentalism.

Can reconvened in 1989 for the one-off, Rite Time. After the implosion of La Düsseldorf, Klaus Dinger's career languished for a decade or so, until 1996 when he formed the mischievously-named group La! Neu?. They recorded three studio albums and two live albums within a couple of years, before Dinger was once again beset by ill health and financial woes. His death in 2008 does not seem to have provoked critics to reassess their condescending attitude to the last phases of his career, but I believe that in the more distant future, La! Neu?'s albums will be recognised as rather special.

A different incarnation of Brainticket featuring one original member issued two albums in the early 1980s. The recording date is uncertain; the music may have been made in the 1970s.

Amon Düül II regrouped in 1995 and produced the creditable *Nada Moonshine #* album. Since then, they have been playing live but have so far produced no fresh material.

Also worth mentioning here is Tangerine Dream, one of the longest-lived of the original German proto-electronica outfits. Julian Cope, in his influential book *Krautrocksampler*, claimed that he lost interest in them after they signed to Virgin in 1973. Few Krautrock lovers would be quite so hard-line, but I've noticed that the most common position is that Tangerine Dream were only really Tangerine Dream until 1977, when they lost Peter Baumann. Thus all the subsequent albums can be conveniently ignored. It's a neat theory but, in truth, the decline of Tangerine Dream was slower and more fitful than this journalistic story allows, and there are some gems floating around in the swill.

Klaus Schulze's evolution parallels Tangerine Dream's. The liner notes of his 1980 *…live…* album announced the end of an old era and the beginning of a new—a convenient point at which purists could cease to follow his career. More open-minded listeners should be able to extract some value from Schulze's voluminous later work. Even so, his 1970s output remains in a different class.

3. "Amon Düül II have moved from being revolutionists to being absolute professionals."

4. A disco-baiting variant on the nineteenth century American military motto "The only good Indian is a dead Indian."

5. "We want to live." Without Eroc, Grobschnitt lasted until the late 1980s. They have recently reformed, if such a word makes sense for a band with just one original member (Wildschwein, the singer) performing oldies for the nostalgia crowd.

6. Guru Guru's Mani Neumeier recently (2007/2008) achieved something like a full circle back to his

anarchist roots when he collaborated with the Krautrock-obsessed Japanese freakout ensemble Acid Mothers Temple for a series of concerts.

7. A good album, too, proving that compromise is not always a bad thing.

8. "Lucky" or "in a state of happiness". "Im Glück" is also the title of a track on the first NEU! album.

8

8 Kraan *Wintrup*, 1972.

BAND PROFILES

Agitation Free in Cairo, 1972. Courtesy Michael Hoenig. Photo: HV Putkammer.

It's hard to believe that a name as apposite as Agitation Free was taken at random from the dictionary, as band members claimed. "Agitation" can mean anything from simple movement to mental disturbance, but in the case of Agitation Free—the latter part of the name added after the group's long-form festival performances—there was more relevance in the subsidiary meaning of ideas being thrown back and forward in debate or discussion. Personnel changed steadily after the group's inception in 1967, sometimes as the result of internal differences (with founding guitarist Lutz Kramer leaving in 1970) or as part of a free exchange of talent with the German experimental music community. In 1970, the group appeared at the First German Progressive Pop Festival at the Sportpalast in Berlin, after which the personnel settled into its most recognisable and distinctive form. The interlocking lines of guitarists Lutz Ulbrich (also associated with Ash Ra Tempel) and Jörg Schwenke, and of founding bassist Michael Günther and keyboardist Michael Hoenig, suggested a band which regarded music as a series of playful quiddities and one that took less interest in political agitation than contemporaries Floh de Cologne or Guru Guru. The latter 'borrowed' bassist Axel Genrich, and forgot to return him, while founding drummer Christoph Franke went to Tangerine Dream and was replaced by Burghard Rausch. The visual dimension provided by multimedia artist Folke Hanfeld was also notably playful and less inclined to agit-prop.

Rather than concentrating on German social reality or a radical critique of the Wirtschaftswunder (or 'economic miracle'), Agitation Free seemed to take at closer to face value chancellor Willy Brandt's challenge to the German young to "dare more". In contrast to the polemical thrust of many of their contemporaries, the group followed a more utopian course, deriving much of their musical inspiration from an ear-opening trawl through the eastern Mediterranean funded by the Goethe Institute. The debut album *Malesch* is a near-perfect representation of Brandt's concept of "extended culture", an intricate musical carpet woven out of free jazz, psychedelia and 'found' recordings made in Egypt and Lebanon. The group performed in the cultural programme of the 1972 Olympiad in Munich, an event notorious for the Black September attacks on Israeli athletes but also notable for an ambitious and eclectic musical programme. By contrast, the unimaginatively titled *2nd* is more song-based and finished in tone, lacking *Malesch*'s hallucinatory shimmer. Major appearances followed throughout Europe, including an important appearance at the prestigious Warsaw Autumn in 1974. A live album was released in 1976, two years after the group disbanded, not so much riven by personal differences as no longer able to hold together the centrifugal interests of individual members. There were later reunions, with assorted personnels, but the Agitation Free story is effectively condensed into half a decade of activity. Its close association with composer Thomas Kessler's Beat Studio in Berlin-Wilmersdorf put it close to artists as varied as John Cage and Ladislav Kupkoviç, and at the heart of the German electronic music scene. Their reciprocal influence continues to this day.
BM

AGITATION FREE

AMON DÜÜL

Despite having been described as "Krautrock's most hated band", despite having been eventually eclipsed by Amon Düül II, their more musically competent and coherent successors, the first incarnation of Amon Düül is a historically vital Krautrock cornerstone. Taking their name from Amon, an Egyptian deity associated with creative force and the championing of the poor and the needy, one might think of Amon Düül as the first sprouting of hair on the adolescent and angry face of German music as it emerged from its beat-pop phase into the Europe-wide counterculture of the late 1960s. They began as a collective, founded by jazz musician Chris Karrer in 1967; based in a house in Munich, they co-established the Krautrock principle that in order to create a new cultural model of playing, being and doing, it would be necessary to remove oneself from society. "We are eleven adults and two children which are gathered to make all kinds of expressions, also musical", announced Karrer, as if to stress that music formed merely a part of the group's rainbow of activities.

Inevitably, the personnel and numbers were in constant flux, numbering maybe ten or 12 at a time, comprising not just musicians but painters and political activists, with honorary affiliates such as Uschi Obermaier, the emergent poster girl of the German underground scene. Other members included Peter Leopold, Ullrich Leopold, Rainer Bauer, Ella Bauer, Helge Filanda, Angelica Filanda, Krischke and Eleonora Romana.

The chronology and discography of Amon Düül is a little confusing. They released four albums between 1969 and 1971 but three of them derive from the same jam session in 1968. They split that year, on the very night that they were invited to play alongside Frank Zappa's Mothers Of Invention and The Fugs at the Internationale Essener Sontage festival, at which Tangerine Dream also played, and which would prove a founding moment for younger members of the Krautrock tradition. It was certainly a founding moment for Amon Düül II, born that night as Chris Karrer and the more musical-minded members of the collective decided to break away from the more amusical, politically orientated faction within the group.

The first Amon Düül album, *Psychedelic Underground*, was released in 1969. The opening track, "Ein Wunderhubsches Madchen Traumt Von Sandosa" is a 17 minute epic which captures the lo-fi, lo-ability exuberant essence of Düül. Percussive-heavy and driven by tribal rhythms and chanting, which almost drown out the rudimentary thrash of acoustic guitar, it's certainly evidence of a group of people who have been having a very, very good time at the commune, experiencing mind expanding substances as well as the rigours of revolutionary political debate. One senses the involvement of body paint. This is probably what Krautrock sounds to untutored, dyspeptic outsiders who think that "all this sort of music sounds the same"—a perversely repetitive, primitive and self-indulgent drone all but dissolving in its own fuzz. And yet, it has about it an undeniably infectious joy and, in its outsider artistry and determined communitarianism, even an implied political component lacking in some of the better wrought Krautrock output. The rest of *Psychedelic Underground* shambles along in a similarly euphoric vein, like a street procession, culminating in "Bitterlings Verwandlung", in which the jamming is buffeted by broadsides of interruption from a classical music channel, an example of the sort of basic but inspired studio manipulation which was characteristic of Amon Düül and which would be followed up in more elaborate ways by subsequent groups like Faust.

Two more albums were culled from these sessions; *Collapsing*, 1969, and *Disaster*, 1971, and, inevitably, both feel cut from the same cloth, though both in spirit militate against their gloomily apocalyptic titles. Again, on *Disaster*'s "Drum Things" for example the feel is rough, raucous and defiant—these are hardly 'Germanic' sounds but could conceivably emanate from say, Brazil or Africa, or any place where seven or so percussionists are assembled. "Asynchron" from the same album uncannily prefigures some of Can's wilder moments on *Tago Mago*, while "Yea Yea Yea (Zerbeatelt)" doesn't so much cover The Beatles' "I Should Have Known Better" as chew it to bits.

A more finished side to Amon Düül was revealed on *Paradieswarts Düül*, released in

1970 in the wake of their initial split. It's a more settled, lucid and pastoral affair, dominated by the bucolic and affirmative tones of the 17 minute long "Love Is Peace" (which also contains the equally sanguine and dubious observation that "Freedom is harmony"). This wheels on through acoustic meadows before eventually ascending to a Heaven of cosmic reverb. "Snow Your Thirst And Sun Your Open Mouth" shows a capable degree of mood shift, from the joyful to the still and introspective. The concluding "Eternal Flow", meanwhile, in its luminous delicacy, reminds of the 1980s UK group AR Kane, who visited similar pastures on their 1988 album 69.

Other albums were subsequently released under the Amon Düül moniker but the beginning of the end occurred not just with the faction breaking away to form II but when they were forced out of their commune in Munich and forced to operate out of a two room apartment. That proved to be too much urban reality for Amon Düül to flourish in. They should not, however, be regarded as a hippy aberration from which Krautrock recovered but as a key and crucial blueprint in its development, whose albums, for all their deficiencies, deservedly command affection and repay reinspection.

DS

AMON DÜÜL II

Mötörhead, Hüsker Dü, Björk, even Brüno: there's a modest thesis to be written about the umlaut as a signifier in popular culture. To Anglo-Saxon eyes, it implies strangeness, a dark exoticism, a subtle element of threat. Which may in part explain the double appeal of Amon Düül II, one of the pioneering German rock bands and an enduring presence on the European scene.

The death of drummer Peter Leopold in 2006 seemed likely to ring down the curtain on the Amon Düül story, but when Leopold was replaced by Daniel Fichelscher, who had worked with the group in earlier days, something of its continuity and communitarian spirit was reaffirmed. The group appears in Rainer Werner Fassbinder's 1970 film *The Niklashausen Journey*, jamming in front of an 'audience' of stoned hippies, alienated love-children, the indulged, neglected progeny of a wartime generation. Like many Krautrock bands, the history of Amon Düül II is inseparable from the political history of post-war Germany, and yet, typically, the group's work expresses a bleakly retrofitted utopianism, a set of dark alternatives to Germany's consumer-driven resurgence and political quietism.

The name both attracts and puzzles, as does the numeral. For a time, the two Amon Düüls coexisted. They had their origins in a Munich art commune, where large-scale collective improvisations or musical happenings were part of the ethos. The group's name was derived from that of the Egyptian sun-god, though there is some dispute over what Düül represents. Some have suggested that he is a character in a Turkish novel; others that it is an arbitrarily chosen name with no significance and no reference to the Gästarbeiter problem. By 1969, the commune was divided into two factions. Amon Düül I gravitated towards long psychedelic jams, three early examples of which were released as LPs. The members of what became Amon Düül II were more technically proficient, instinctively resistant to the anti-technique of the fellow-communards, and arguably more interested in public recognition, if not commercial success.

Amon Düül I's music is of historical interest, but rarely discussed other than in that context. Amon Düül II came to wider notice with the release in 1969 of the group's first record *Phallus Dei*. Again, the title alone—"God's Cock"!—was guaranteed to attract attention and almost at once the group became a cult favourite. The sound, similar in some regards to early Can, relied on overlayered guitars, insistent but not always metrical percussion, and vocals that had an indefinable public address quality, as if calling the audience to a ritual or political event. Lothar Meid's eerie falsetto, with Renate Knaup-Kroetenschwanz vocalising wordlessly behind, gave the group an instantly recognisable focus. Other key members were Peter Leopold, bassist Dave Anderson, guitarist Chris Karrer, bassist/keyboardist Falk U Rogner, and multi-instrumentalist John Weinzierl. Several members doubled on other instruments, including saxophones, which helped sustain a sometimes awkwardly integrated jazz feel to Amon Düül II.

Indeed, the constituent elements of *Phallus Dei* only start to combine with the long title track. The opening "Kanaan" is resonant prog, a brilliant fanfare for nascent Krautrock. What follows, "Dem Güten, Schönen, Währen", could hardly be a greater contrast, a beerfest version of the Sun Ra Arkestra. "Luzifers Ghilom" is A-rated psychedelia, an edgy folk rock that still carries a power to disturb. "Henriette Kroetenschwanz" again hints at elements of German vernacular culture, but in a fragmentary and confusing way that heightens the song's personal charge. "Phallus Dei" resonates for its entire 20-minute duration, a monumental slice of improvisatory rock.

Critics must have been tempted to accept the cue and dismiss the sequel *Yeti* as "abominable". In reality, it's the stronger record, and a similar mix of long-form improvisation and more straightforwardly structured songs. It marks the appearance of "Archangel Thunderbird", which became the signature Knaup performance. "Cerberus" was another folk-inspired piece, whose components re-emerged elsewhere in improvisation. "Soap Shop Rock", as vividly declaratory an opening track as "Kanaan" was on the first album, is arguably more individual and better representative of the group's sound. Even allowing for some molten guitar-playing on *Yeti*, there were no very distinctive instrumentalists in Amon Düül II. The group's character is in the interplay.

Tanz der Lemminge was a more reflective record. Long continuous pieces, or rather sequences of themes, made up three of the original double-LP sides. "Syntelman's March of the Roaring Seventies" confirms the undercurrent of satire that makes Amon Düül's music more playful and joyous than most fans and critics were prepared to acknowledge at the time or since. "Restless Twilight—Transistor Child" is angrier and more fragmentary in approach, but there are clear signs of underlying structure and dramatic direction, an indication that Weinzierl, Rogner and Karrer (arguably the main composers) were not simply anarchic tricksters but radical formalists as well.

Despite the free-for-all of "Hawknose Harlequin", *Carnival in Babylon* was a song album, cast in relatively unadventurous forms and with every sense that Amon Düül had settled into a 'style'.

That was confirmed by *Wolf City*, also released in 1972. Experimental elements were too obviously superadded and no longer seemed the driving force. By the end of the decade, perhaps in tandem with a steadily declining political situation, the group's energies were largely dissipated, though *Hijack* (a loaded term in 1974) took some pains to resist the ossification. *Made in Germany* from the following year made fun of 'music as product' but the shift to Atlantic Records had confirmed that that was precisely what Amon Düül II had become. The group disbanded in 1981.

Weinzierl and Anderson (who'd been part of the Hawkwind collective) attempted to revive the group as Amon Düül UK, a title which either missed or underlined the pointlessness of the exercise; it might have worked as 'ÜK' in an earlier decade! There have been later revivals as nostalgia for the 1970s underground became big business, but no one was looking for any fresh insights or for a return to the original group's bizarre mix of psychedelic doodling and iron-hard melodic invention. Frequently cited alongside Can as one of the monoliths of Krautrock, Amon Düül II never quite overcame a lumpiness of vision or the tension between their own libertarian instincts and the centripetal pull of the music business.

BM

Courtesy Eurock Archives.

Mention "a group called Anima" to any number of music fans and you might find yourself scoring ten for ten, only to discover that no two are thinking about the same band. It's probably the most over-used group name of all, attracting Turkish heavy metallers, Indonesians, classical ensembles, Hondurans, New Agers and Latin-dance lovers, not all of whom necessarily know anything about Jung. None of the many outfits to use Anima as a title quite so profoundly plumbed the collective unconscious of middle Europe at the turn of the 1960s as the married couple Paul and Limpe Fuchs, who also went out as Anima-Sound.

Unlike most groups of the period, who seemed to come and go in a moment, the Fuchses carried on their explorations for decades, eventually going out as a trio with their son, and for a time as Limpe Fuchs' solo act, the latter appearing as the widow and relict of the 1960s avant-garde, no longer nude in black body paint but still a living mourner for a lost past. In reality, Anima-Sound didn't slip out of time because they were never quite in it, having rejected their peers' generational conflicts almost entirely in favour of a self-made aesthetic that had no ties to commercial culture and a willingness to confront positively the representatives of an older—or more 'official'—generation in German culture.

The couple struck up an association with the rather older Austrian-born composer and pianist Friedrich Gulda, whose own career was intriguingly split between Bach-and-Mozart classicism and a commitment to both free music and the new vernacular of pop and rock. His best-known composition was a set of variations on "Light My Fire" by Robbie Krieger of The Doors. Paul and Limpe Fuchs recorded with Gulda in 1972, a year which also saw him record *Book One* of *Das Wohltemperierte Klavier* and tour with Weather Report, a fair indication of his eclecticism.

Anima's *Musik für Alle* philosophy was reflected in an imaginative use of homemade instruments—described as *Fuchshorn*, *Fuchszither* and so on—as a complement to Limpe's vivid but untutored drumming and wordless vocalising, and Paul's gloriously declamatory cornet and horn playing. Fragmentary footage of the two suggests music of an ecstatic cast that doesn't

ANIMA/ PAUL AND LIMPE FUCHS

entirely carry over onto record. The first
album *Stürmischer Himmel* was recorded
privately in a remote location and released
on Ohr in 1971. The previous year, the
couple had appeared in a 'documentary'
entitled *Sex Freedom in Germany*, a nicely
camouflaged exploitation film memorable for
Limpe in her body paint.

The group created a stir at Gulda's 1972
Ossiach Festival and made two discs with
him. Further records followed through the
1970s, including Monte Alto and the double
It's Up To You—which finds the group aesthetic
(a curious mix of psychedelic folk, Carl
Orff amateur music making and AACM 'little
instruments' improvisation) stretched to
breaking point. By the end of the decade,
Paul and Limpe were joined by son Zoro
Fuchs, but the addition of a 'regular'
drummer codified the music uncomfortably.
In later years, Limpe continued as a solo
performer, restoring the ecstatic simplicity
and verveful adventure of early days.

BM

Limpe Fuchs live in 1977. Courtesy Limpe Fuchs.

ASH RA TEMPEL

Despite various name changes, personnel shifts and members dropping dramatically to earth, Ash Ra Tempel represent a continuum from the Ur-rock of the Velvet Underground and MC5 and space rock of Pink Floyd to the ambient soundscapes of the present day.

They started life as an altogether earthier proposition: the Steeple Chase Bluesband, formed in 1969 and featuring Manuel Göttsching (guitar), Hartmut Enke (bass) and Wulf Arp (drums). They earned their spurs doing cover versions by "blues explosion" 1960s artists like John Mayall. However, in 1970, Göttsching and Enke met Klaus Schulze in Berlin and they undertook a series of rehearsals, consisting largely of lengthy improvisations in which they untethered themselves from their musical pasts and took flight, at once inspired by and rejecting the example of Anglo-American rock.

Their first, self-titled album, produced by Conny Plank, was released in 1971 and is regarded as a key fixture in the kosmische firmament. Borne aloft on a crest of cymbals, opening track "Amboss" is a sustained, cirrus trail of guitar whose hankering, exploratory tones have yet to be superseded,

even in the post-rock era. Remotely serene, distantly turbulent, it does echo Pink Floyd's *Ummagumma* for sure, but takes up where the live half of that album left off. "Traummaschine" is a more troubled affair, initially beatless and hardly there except for the cries of angels in exile, before a percussive momentum takes it off into another quadrant.

However, the turn of the 1970s was a fast-moving time for Krautrock, full of unbound potential energy, and so it was that Klaus Schulze departed Ash Ra Tempel to pursue his solo destiny. For their second, underrated album *Schwingungen*, Tempel brought on board a raft of guest musicians, including singer John L, whose breathy, wavering vocals on "Light And Darkness: Light" had an unmistakable pharmaceutical dimension to them. Compared to its predecessor, *Schwingungen* sounds more mired in the blues swamplands from which Ash Ra Tempel had first emerged—however, as Hendrix had already shown, there is a logical trajectory between blues and space rock and it's one followed up by Manuel Göttsching here. This is the blues refried, ingested, used as fuel for a much further reaching

Brian Barritt and members of Ash Ra Tempel crew during recording of *7UP*.

Ash Ra Tempel and Timothy Leary, 1972. Courtesy Brian Barritt.

exploration which eventually reaches the galactic stasis of "Light And Darkness" and the vibes-soaked, percussive meteor showers of "Suche And Liebe".

Ash Ra Tempel's next phase would make them part of acid rock legend, as they embarked on a project with American LSD guru Timothy Leary, who had escaped from an American jail, fled the country on a false passport and was currently in exile in Switzerland, darting from canton to canton and, in middle age, his marriage collapsed, embarking on a reckless spree of adventures, largely pharmaceutical. Ash Ra Tempel had intended to make an album with sometime beat poet Allen Ginsberg but were stymied by the fact that Ginsberg was not at hand. However, word reached Harmut Enke that Timothy Leary was, just over the border in Switzerland, experimenting with heroin and supposedly "communicating telepathically" with his friend Brian Barritt.

Enke and Leary met up, the young bassist immersing himself for a while in the world of the old American hand. Leary proposed a concept for a new album, based around a "mind map" which would take you through the stages of perception, culminating eventually in the supreme condition, the "white light" at which point you can go no further as consciousness and identity dissolve. A fresh raft of musicians were drafted in to help realise this concept musically, and the resultant album, an uneasy mixture of phases and styles from the ethereal to the blues-raucous, was entitled 7UP, in honour of the fact that Leary's son in law, Dennis Martino at one point spiked the group's soft drinks with acid during the proceedings.

The album, on which Leary contributed vocals was to everybody's surprise a one-off, as Leary fell victim to homesickness for America, where he eventually returned and served a brief period in jail. As for

Enke, it is probably no coincidence that after prolonged fraternisation with Leary and his people, he burned out, in a single, dramatic moment, onstage in 1973, in the middle of a concert in Cologne. He stopped playing, sat down, wreathed in smiles, declaring himself happy just to be listening to the beautiful music going on around him rather than participating. He has not participated in music making since.

Prior to this, however, he did play on 1972's *Join Inn*, which saw the temporary return of Klaus Schulze. This was a jam session that arose from studio hours waiting for musicians to turn up to play on Walter Wegmüller's legendary *Tarot* album.

Since the mid-1970s, Ash Ra Tempel has become practically synonymous with the solo work of Manuel Göttsching. 1974's *Inventions For Electric Guitar*, featuring the loping arpeggios of "Pluralis" systematically subjects the instrument to

numerous treatments such as looping and delay, a more compact, minimalist approach to 'progressive guitar' which was also being practised to different effect by Steve Hillage and Robert Fripp. In 1977, Ash Ra Tempel became Ashra, and the title of the album they produced that year, *New Age Earth*, might have seemed out of kilter with punk sensibilities but foreshadowed pre-occupations of the 1990s. This was true also of 1984's *E2-E4*, whose gently scampering, static odyssey of electronics sounds like the staple post-rave fare of a decade later, as taken up by the likes of System 7 and The Orb. Göttsching, then, has been hailed as a "godfather of trance", though for many it is the remote and unparalleled analogue space rock journeys he and Tempel made in the 1970s which are crying out to be revisited, resumed and extended.

DS

Ash Ra Tempel and crew (including Rolf-Ulrich Kaiser, Gille Lettmann, Timothy Leary, Sergius Golowin, and Klaus D Mueller). Courtesy Eurock Archives. Photo: Marcel Fugere.

PLASTIC CRIMEWAVE
ON ASH RA TEMPEL AND THE COSMIC COURIERS

I guess it all started with classic rock—Floyd, Sabbath and Hendrix led me to Syd, Nuggets and the Velvets—and then I was hooked on psychedelia. Trading fourth generation tapes with older collectors was my only hope for finding then-out-of-print psych monsters. Finally I happened upon a dub of the first Ash Ra Tempel LP, and not much could have prepared me for the lengthy tracks that took up this cassette side. The first cut whipped up into a freewheeling and raging storm, while the second was pure liquid ambience. My chemical-addled head was forever rearranged—this charging DIY-energy stab at seemingly improvisational, devotional acid rock (it wasn't till way later that I saw the Egyptian-derived fold out cover, when I was given an original copy) took off where the 1960s had left off in Britain and the US. It soon became painfully obvious that the aforementioned Floyd and Velvets had tamed their initial explorations into well-produced songs as time went on, and generally everyone got more laid back in the 1970s, while the Germans picked up the freak-flag torch, and taken it further out. Soon I dug up other albums like *Schwingungen* and *Join Inn*, and things did become slightly more refined, as a sparser, more phased approach settled in, with chanting vocals and more space leaking in—it all especially influenced my approach to the guitar as textural landscape provider. Ash Ra would lead me to other members of their Cosmic Courier family—the even more blissed-out and devotional Sergius Golowin, the excessive supergroup space-glam of Walter Wegmüller's *Tarot*, and most importantly the Cosmic Jokers and Witthüser & Westrupp. Cosmic Jokers informed me of the possibilities of a patchwork, dub-like approach to recording only hinted at in groups like Can or Guru Guru. Speaking of Can, when I played the sadly-deceased guitarist Michael Karoli a Witthüser & Westrupp track at an interview in 1997, he seemed confused that I was into such "traditional German music"—but to me, these were totally exotic sounds unlike any other I'd heard—their *Trips und Träume* LP truly took me "somewhere else" like any good music should. From this record I learned the possibilities inherent in so-called "acid folk" music. Delay, delay, reverb and even more spiraling delay and reverb over gorgeous melodies and gently pitched electronics (like if Popol Vuh had been more into Richard Thompson) blew my little mind, and shaped the way I would hear recordings in my head before going into the studio—I even nabbed my friend Sisca to speak a poem I'd written in German for my first "solo album" (yup, still unreleased) ala a track on *Trips*.

Of all the new generation German bands, Between were one of the most unique and progressive musically. Founded in 1970 by Peter Michael Hamel, using the name "Between the Chairs", the other core members throughout were Roberto Dêtree (an Argentinean guitarist) and Robert Eliscu (a former symphony member on oboe). They were joined by various percussionists and other jazz/ethnic accompanists in concert and on recordings.

Hamel himself was the musical visionary behind the group. He studied with Karlheinz Stockhausen and was influenced by Cage, Glass, Reich and Terry Riley. He also traveled to India extensively and studied the works of Jung along with other spiritual and psychological writings.

As a group Between (the name having been shortened) fused all their various talents, experiences and philosophy along with instrumental virtuosity together to create five albums—*Einsteig*, 1971, *And the Waters Opened*, 1973, *Dharana*, 1974, *Hesse Between Music* (spoken word texts with music), 1975, and *Contemplation*, 1977. Back then, and still to this day they contained some of the most adventurous and inspirational examples of deeply powerful worldly music you will hear. At the end of the 1970s Between as a band ceased to exist.

Parallel to the group's work, and after their demise, Hamel made some ten solo recordings up until the early 1990s. Of them all, the albums *Hamel*, 1970, *Nada*, 1977, and *Bardo*, 1981, highlight the depth of his talents along with the roots and branches of the style he was exploring musically. They are a creative wonder, illustrating wonderfully his deeply spiritual essence and compositional gifts as well.

In 1976, Hamel published his book *Through Music to the Self* describing the connection music has to inner life and the pathway it opens up to a deeper understanding and experience of life holistically. He also continued with his own music: composing during the 1980s–90s most notably four operas, writing scores for string quartets as well as performing on piano, prepared piano, pipe organ, voice and electronics.

In 1997, Hamel succeeded György Ligeti as a professor of composition at the school for Music and Theater in Hamburg. His music has also been performed in various places by noted symphony orchestras and musicians over the last decade. Undoubtedly he was and still is one of the most talented of all the original German musicians remaining creative musically today.

AP

BETWEEN/ PETER MICHAEL HAMEL

CAN

"The individual ideas of the individual
Can members have nothing in common",
declared Can during a 1971 interview for
German television. And so it was, for a
group whose members were each, in their
own way, a "wild card". Keyboardist Irmin
Schmidt was classically trained but also a
lover of John Cage and it was his sudden
interventions which were liable to alter
the entire flow, colour and direction of a
Can jam. Holger Czukay, always a Salvador
Dalínian twinkle in his eye, was tight
to the point of invisibility on bass at
times but also introduced to the group the
outside, subverting elements of shortwave
radio transmissions and prototype samples,
and played as effectively on the instrument
of scissors in the editing suite. Guitarist
Michael Karoli, the most youthful member
of the group offered the most conventional
connection to a wider rock audience but
his playing was tinged with his love of
Eastern European folk and gypsy music. As
for drummer Jaki Liebezeit, he came from
a free jazz background yet, perversely,
baulked at the liberties such music afforded
him, yearning for the straitjacket of a
more cyclical, repetitive mode of playing.
Add into this mix first Malcolm Mooney—a
sculptor from New York gone AWOL in Europe,
who ended up internalising the looped chaos
of Can to heart and had to leave the group
for the sake of his mental health—then Damo
Suzuki—an ex-busker whose featherweight,
improvised vocals enabled Can to take to the
air—and you have one of the most perfectly
integrated collectives in rock history.

Debuting in 1968, Can, like other
Krautrock collectives, withdrew into their
own playing and rehearsal space, Schloss
Nörvenich outside Cologne, in order to work
up an identity that was free of the malign
influences that inhibited German ersatz
beat music in the 1960s, making music as
if they were the first people ever to do
so. In calling their studios Inner Space,
they further exacerbated this sense of
introversion. And yet, their influences were
themselves Anglo-American, particularly US
garage rock and the studied primitivism
of the Velvet Underground, whom they used
as milestones on the journey back to first
principles. The name "Can" was later
suggested by Liebezeit to have stood for

"Communism, Anarchism, Nihilism" but it had other effective connotations which all fit too—metal, cylindrical, conceptual in a Warholian sense (as displayed on the 1972 album *Ege Bamyasi*), as well as a declaration of infinite potential.

Can's earliest albums, such as 1968's *Delay*, have a primordial, riffing feel to them, belonging both to a notional future but also a new 'stone age' for a new mode of rock. They were the products of hours and hours of jamming, worked down into minimal but heavy, remorselessly exploratory workouts, in which the character of each player comes to the fore despite an avowed lack of interest in 'personal expression'—on tracks like "Pnoom", the greater sum of the whole is all.

With the departure of Mooney, however, and the recruitment of the physically and vocally slight Damo Suzuki in his place, Can began to sound like less of a liquid than a solid preposition, ranging more freely across the sound universe, even raising the odd smile. "Aumgn", from 1971's *Tago Mago* is like a Journey to the Centre of the Head, with violins, guitar and keyboards surfing the reverb and vocals resounding through the mix as if from a giant larynx. This is a group unmoored, exploring realms beyond the bounds of soloing and interplay. This new Can, with their new "lightness of being" was further exemplified on *Ege Bamyasi*, with Jaki Liebezeit's playing in particular now giving the group as a whole a floating, gravity-defying sensation on tracks like "Spoon". Liebezeit's near-homicidal determination in the studio to reduce Czukay's bass in the mix undoubtedly added to this.

1973's *Future Days* saw Can ascend to yet another zenith; the title track and the lengthy "Bel Air" play out in a sort of drowsy, blazing, Utopian haze, as if Can had found their own planet upon which to play, with its own, musical climate. Suzuki thrives, Aeriel-like, on this particular album, wafting about, butterfly-like. However, it also contains "Moonshake", a rigid, rhythmical portent of the shape of dance rhythms to come.

Suzuki departed Can, however, and became a Jehovah's witness, and with 1974's *Soon Over Babaluma*, Can decided to operate as a mostly instrumental four piece. For some, this was the beginning of Can's end but *Babaluma* has some exceptional moments, which foretell some of the content of Talking Heads' much more widely heard *Remain In Light*, released six years later. 1975's *Landed* marked a further decline for some, although a track

like "Red Hot Indians", with its abstract synth chatter is in the group's best traditions, while the lengthy "Unfinished" is like a piece of latter-day musique concrète and a reminder of the group's origins in that department—Holger Czukay was a pupil of Stockhausen.

Thereafter, Can did decline—personnel introductions and changes, such as the gradual ousting of Holger Czukay, fatally altered the delicate chemistry of the group. Perversely, they had a hit of sorts with 1976's proto-disco "I Want More", even appearing on Top Of The Pops, but commercial gambits like this couldn't rescue them from decline.

And yet, far from slipping into irrelevance, Can were almost as active a force in their afterlife, following their late 1970s split, as they had been during their years as an operative unit. Their influence on punk and post-punk was avidly declared by John Lydon, Pete Shelley and Mark E Smith among others. Solo ventures saw the group very much at the leading edge rather than adding mere footnotes to spent careers. Jaki Liebezeit and Holger Czukay worked with PiL's Jah Wobble on the brilliant EP "How Much Are They?". With his 1980 album *Movies*, Holger Czukay wittily prefigured the decade's later move towards sampling with "Cool In The Pool", and, with "Persian Love", continued Can's tongue in cheek love affair with world music (as evinced on their Ethnological Forgery series). Irmin Schmidt made, with Bruno Spoerri, the album *Toy Planet*, whose

"Rapido De Noir" in particular demonstrated the cinematic capabilities of Can.

Can reformed one last time in 1989 for the album *Rite Time*, with Malcolm Mooney turning up out of the blue to record with them. *Rite Time* was a timelessly respectable addition to their canon. Band members met and worked together intermittently or in tandem, regrouping again in 1997 to promote an album of dance remixes of their work. It was a reminder that Can have been and remain an unlikely and continuing touchstone, from post-punk to post-rock, from dance to world music. Their combination of rigid minimalism and flow motion (Can are a group who simultaneously "go" nowhere yet get everywhere) is yet another example of the way Krautrock reconfigured the music of times past, present and to come.

DS

Can with Malcom Mooney (far right) in Zürich, 1968. Courtesy Spoon Records.

ANN SHENTON ON
CAN AND DAMO SUZUKI

The fact that Damo Suzuki was allegedly picked up by the band while busking has always attracted me to the ethics of Can—a street performer became the bands' front man. This says to me that there were not the normal egos in tow, and that Can approached the band set up differently—in a more fluid and inventive way. This attitude was something that me and my band were attempting when we first began performing in the early 1990s.

When I recently played as a sound carrier for Suzuki in his Never Ending Tour, I dusted down my old Moog Rogue, and headed off to meet Suzuki and the rest of the 'temporary band'. I was interested in his method of orchestration or non method as the case may be. During our sound check a young enthusiast wanted to write up a set list and plan the performance in greater depth but Suzuki was totally against that. We had to communicate in real time, as we were playing, with no pre planning. In his experience the pre planned stuff never works as well as the impromptu playing and anyway our time could be better spent nipping to the Japanese café and sampling the sake. Good idea.

Suzuki reacts to the vibrations of the moment, not a set of pre meditated rules. During the performance a simple nod, a flick of his mane or a drum roll would signify a change of pace—we would react on the fly like starlings in the evening sky changing direction in synch. Then he was off to the next gig in Paris; he's a real modern day nomad singing for his supper.

The words "Ege Bamyasi" so Suzuki told me was something Can saw scrawled on the menu in a Turkish café, it made no sense to them at the time, and it doesn't mean anything to me either it but sounds good; a great readymade album title in true Dadaist style. When you take into account that Suzuki was singing in Japanese, German or English, the words didn't always mean anything or make sense to the listener, so by randomly taking those words Can were reinforcing the concept of the voice as sound making device, and that non sense could in fact make a lot of sense, like the cut ups of William Burroughs and the Surrealists with their exquisite corpse game.

I just wish I had seen Can live, but like loads of bands I'm into I was too young to experience them in real time, when Can were out gigging I was going to see ABBA & Alvin Stardust. It's the only time I wish I was a pensioner.

CLUSTER

Kluster emerged from the Zodiak Free Arts Lab, a music venue run by Conrad Schnitzler and Hans-Joachim Roedelius in the back room of the Schaubühne theatre-bar in late 1960s West Berlin. Here freaks and avant-gardists of all stripes could enjoy live psychedelia, free jazz, free performance and freakout; it was a venue, a practice space and, as the birthing ground for both Tangerine Dream (Schnitzler was a founder member) and Kluster, a galactic centre for kosmische musik.

In-house performances came from Schnitzler's 'chamber' groups Noises and Plus/Minus and the eight-piece sonic gestalt group Human Being, featuring Roedelius, who also performed solo with "a microphone, a hand-made flute and an alarm clock". Amongst the Lab's regulars was Dieter Moebius. One evening in mid-July 1969 Conny and Achim, as they were known, asked Moebius to join a group called Kluster. A few days later the trio were playing a 12-hour concert in a gallery above a Berlin shopping centre.

Early performances were always improvised (as were all the albums produced by Kluster, Cluster and, for that matter, most of the true kosmische groups) with the trio employing modified cellos, guitars, flutes, microphones, tape machines, organs, percussion and whatever else they could find to open up new doorways to otherness. Although the small audiences to their first Berlin gigs were largely enthusiastic, within a few months they had relocated themselves, their equipment and their girlfriends to Düsseldorf, where Schnitzler was able to fix them up with more gallery and artspace shows. Kluster were also now ready to record.

Funding for the studio session that produced their first two albums *Klopfzeichen* ('tapping' or 'knocking' signals) and *Zwei-Osterei* (Two Easter Eggs) came from Oskar Gottlieb Blarr, a church organist with a passion for avant-garde music. The records were released on the religious Schwann label, with the proviso that they contained Christian content; hence the first sides of both albums are accompanied by dramatically declaimed agit-poetry and portentious spiritual admonition. Keeping with the religious metaphor, it might be fair to describe the initial Kluster albums as an LSD-dipped tour through the circles of post-war hell: car batteries buzz, oil barrels clang and marbles

roll around in a bowl, accompanied by cello, flute, guitar feedback and organ drones, to create a seething topographic dissonance that stretches from Edgar Varèse on one horizon to the Velvet Underground on the other. This potential audio catastrophe was engineered by the young Conrad "Conny" Plank, who had previously worked with Varèse and was able to give shape and form to Kluster's dense, deep and highly abstract sound. Moebius and Roedelius both refer to the late Plank as a third member of Cluster, and a dear friend.

By 1971 Kluster were beginning to make a name for themselves on the underground, but Schnitzler was ready to pursue life as a solo musician and artist. Moebius and Roedelius, however, were just getting started. The change in line-up required a new name, but their attitude, and their sound, remained much the same. So Kluster became Cluster and, along with their now-friend Conny and a mongrel dog named Stinky, they continued in their mission. Their first album, *Cluster*, was released by Philips, who were quick to get hip with West Germany's newly evolving kosmische sound, and presented the trio (Plank produced once again) evolving at a glacial pace. *Cluster* is, if anything, even darker than its predecessors, with a harsher, more abrasive and electronic sound evoking colossal forges

and tectonic shifts. *Cluster II*, recorded for Brain, transfers the field of operation from the bowels of the Earth into the cold, dark eternity of outer space.

Living out of a van and gigging intensely and extensively—including an unlikely, uncomfortable night at Germany's first open air rock festival, Insel Fehmarn, where Jimi Hendrix gave his final performance—was beginning to take its toll on the dissonant duo, with drugs and alchohol becoming a regular part of their line-up. Relief came in 1971, when Roedelius and Moebius were invited to join an intentional community that had taken over a village, Forst, in the wooded idyll of Lower Saxony.

The first album to be recorded at Forst was 1974's *Zuckerzeit*, a dose of sugary sweetness completely at odds with anything that the group had produced up to that time. Erupting with wonky electronic grooves and ecstatic melodies, it's the seeding ground for myriad future musics and a clear reflection of their idyllic living circumstances. Although Michael Rother was credited in the album's back sleeve as co-producer, the truth was rather different. While Rother was recording *NEU!75* at Conny Plank's studio in Cologne, Cluster were in Forst recording *Zuckerzeit* and using some of Rother's Farfisa instruments

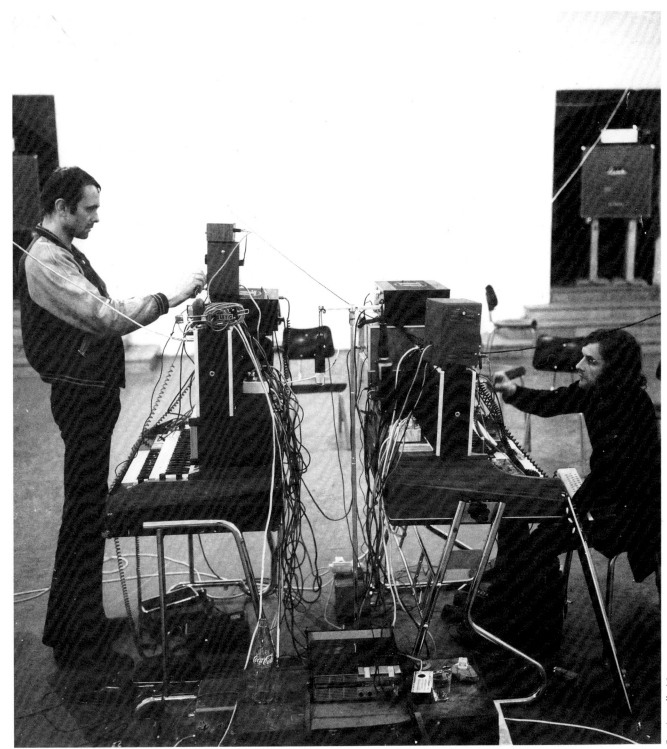

Courtesy Moebius.

and recording gear (his 4-track and Revox stereo master machine). The credit was an acknowledgement of Rother's indirect yet vital contribution.

In 1976, between recording sessions as Harmonia, now with another Forst-visitor, Brian Eno, Cluster recorded *Sowiesoso*, a beautiful, emotionally-satisfying album put together in only two days. The tracks here are more fluid and lengthy than those on *Zuckerzeit*, and their best moments are, if anything, even more beautiful and engaging.

The following two years saw more recording sessions with Brian Eno, this time at Conny Plank's Hamburg studio, with guesting from Can's Holger Czukay and Asmus Tietchens. These sessions gave rise to *Cluster and Eno*, 1977 and *After the Heat*, 1978, two albums of gentle, motive ambience that fall somewhere between the stools of both artists' other work but remain of great interest, particularly "The Belldog", which hints at the more satisfying results that further collaborations might have led to. It's probably fair to say that Cluster (and Harmonia, with whom Eno also recorded) left a greater musical impression on Eno than he did on them, with reworked tracks from these sessions appearing on *Before and After Science*, and also the *Apollo* album.

Two more albums followed these, Grosses Water, 1979, produced by Peter Baumann, formerly of Tangerine Dream, and *Curiosum* in 1981. The former contains some more abrasive pieces reminiscent of their days with Conrad Schnitzler; the latter is a collection of abstractions and melodies. After a few years' hiatus, the duo reformed for an album, *Apropos Cluster* in 1990 and, coinciding with US and Japanese tours in the mid-1990s, *One Hour* in 1995. As of 2007, Moebius and Roedelius are once again playing live, with gigs in Europe and the US.

To listen to Cluster is to undertake a strange adventure through times, sounds and spaces that can, by their improvisational nature, never exist again. Their best music seems to be composed entirely of curious juxtapositions—bold simplicity and fiendish complexity, atonal dissonance and harmonious beauty, elegant sophistication and pratfall foolishness—contrasts perhaps personified in Roedelius and Moebius themselves.

MP

In their own way, Cosmic Jokers are the most remarkable rock group of all time. For even as they jammed away collectively, pushing back the envelope of drone and stoner rock so far that it touched the fringe of psychedelic funk and dub, they had no idea they were a group and no idea that five albums would be made under their name. The joke, in a sense, was on the players, who included Manuel Göttsching of Ash Ra Tempel and Klaus Schulze and none of them, especially Schulze, found it at all funny. For each of the five albums they were involved in—all of which were released in 1974—were recorded by Rolf-Ulrich Kaiser of Kosmische Musik, in an act of extraordinary hubris perpetrated on the artists under his charge which was Malcolm McLarenesque in a way that McClaren himself could only have dreamt of.

The scheme was this. Kaiser would invite the musicians, whose number also included Jürgen Dollase and Harald Grosskopf of Wallenstein, to so-called "acid parties" at the studio of Dieter Dierks, who was also a participant in the recordings. In exchange for jamming, the musicians were

Gille Lettmann. Courtesy of Eurock Archives.

offered drugs, which doubtless deserved a credit of their own on the sleeve insofar as they contributed to the results. Kaiser would then take the tapes and edit them down into album's length recordings, sometimes overdubbed with, for example, spoken word recordings from Kaiser's girlfriend Gille Lettmann on the album *Gilles Zeitschiff* ("Gille's Timeship").

The first to discover what was afoot was Göttsching, who one day walked into a record store in Berlin, and, intrigued by the electro-charged space rock emanating from the shop's sound system, asked who the album was by. He was told it was the latest from Cosmic Jokers, and, to his astonishment, was presented with a sleeve featuring a press shot of himself. The music which so intrigued him had been taken from a jam session in which he himself had taken part just one month earlier.

Despite being broke and not a little angry, Göttsching left the task of protesting at Kaiser's exploitation to Klaus Schulze, who had never cared for the company boss in the first place. Once Schulze initiated proceedings, the game was up, the flow of Cosmic Jokers albums was stemmed forever and Kaiser himself was ruined and forced into exile.

However, there is a strong argument that, despite his 'villainy' and the small matter of proper payment and contractual terms for services offered, Kaiser did lovers of Krautrock a very great service indeed. For by stealth and careful selection in the editing suite, he elicited from Göttsching, Schulze et al, synergetic performances which otherwise would never have come to pass or seen the light of day. Uninhibited by any conceptual brief, or song structures, Cosmic Jokers, their sensibilities altered, expanded and frazzled, hoisted their freak flag high into orbit. This was the music for which the words "far" and "out" should truly have been reserved. The second album, *Galactic Supermarket*, was dominated by the galactic spirals of Jürgen Dollase's mellotron. There then followed *Sci-Fi Party*, a red-editing job presented as a Kosmische Musik sampler and featuring new pieces such as Brian Barritt's "The Electronic Scene". As a friend of Timothy Leary's, Barritt's involvement in this particular scene was unfortunate as it enhanced later accusations that the innocent bloom of Krautrock's youth had been corrupted by the arrival of Leary and his depraved, orgiastic LSD merchants in Europe. As if taunting the musicians inadvertently responsible for these albums, each sleeve featured unauthorised photographs of them in a variety of postures. Next up in very quick succession was *Planeten Sit-In*, which, just to ratchet up the cheek factor, was released in conjunction with a magazine as a quadraphonic demonstration record. Again, though, the standard is high, with jams taking up where Pink Floyd in the rough but spaced out Syd Barrett era left off. Only with the fifth and final album, *Gilles Zeitschiff*, in which the band who had no idea they existed found themselves playing backing to Kaiser's girlfriend, did their patience come to an end.

It was legally and morally just that the story end thus. However, for today's burgeoning generation of stoner rockers, as abundant as weeds particularly on the West Coast of America, the Cosmic Jokers remain a touchstone. Not so much a case of the last laugh as the laugh that has lasted and lasted.

DS

Gille Lettmann, circa 1973. Courtesy of Eurock Archives.

EMBRYO

Billie Holiday and Krautrock: how many degrees of separation? There's a nice change from Kevin Bacon in that old parlour game. The answer, surprisingly, is only two. Lady Day's last accompanist was Mal Waldron, who in his days as an exile in Munich also played with progressive rockers Embryo. The group was formed a decade after Holiday's death, and immediately put out strange fruit. *Opal*, released in 1970, is a psychedelic masterpiece whose best track "End of Soul" seems to follow a similar arc to Soul/Xhol Caravan's germanisation of American r'n'b: Mötöwn, perhaps? Even more interesting in retrospect is the long 'bonus' jam "Läuft" which appeared on the reissue. Here, more of the group's later, ethnically charged language appears in, one's tempted to say "embryo", sketchy form, buried underneath a swirling prog mix.

Drummers Christian Burchard and Dieter Serfas had met in childhood in Hof on the Austrian border, but the group emerged later in Munich, with violinist/saxophonist Edgar Hoffman, guitarists Roman Bunka and Chris Karrer (who also doubled on violin and saxophone) as key members. Essentially,

though, the group was Burchard's; it relied on a vast, rolling pool of musicians and guests from jazz and world music, including Waldron, saxophonist Charlie Mariano and multi-instrumentalist Trilok Gurtu.

The Indian connection implicit in those latter names was confirmed in 1979 when the group made a pilgrimage to the sub-continent, documented in a fascinating movie called *Vagabunden Karawane*; the habit of travel/research/performance in situ was a fruitful constant. Stylistically, Burchard is certainly a vagabond, taking musical elements from wherever he finds them and fusing them with a confidence and vision that transcends the rapidly varying personnel and instrumentation. The group's appearance at the ill-fated Munich Olympiad in 1972 was the prelude to an evolving multiculturalism. Later that year, the group received sponsorship for a study visit and tour of North Africa, where, like Ornette Coleman, they discovered radically new—or traditionally old—harmonic possibilities in Moroccan music. *Embryo's Rache* (it means revenge, as Sherlock Holmes readers will know) was released in 1971,

Embryo in the studio, 1971. © Uta Hofmann. Courtesy Christian Burchard.

already punctuated with 'ethnic' elements, though the only revenge was enjoyed by the different traditions Burchard pillaged, all of which sounded more interesting in miniature than they did mixed into Embryo's psychedelic collage.

Steig Aus and *Rocksession* from late 1970 and 1971 both featured Waldron, whose dark, minor-feel tonalities anchor the mature Embryo sound. On "Radio Marrakesch" and "Orient Express" from the former record, the group sounds tight and coherent, with Hoffman's violin and Jimmy Jackson's organ the key elements. *We Keep On* is the group's acknowledged masterpiece. The addition of Mariano opened up a spice box of jazz flavours and zingy ethnic top-notes and Bunka, co-composer of the delicious "Ehna, Ehna, Abu Lele", completes the hybridisation process. The title track is an extraordinary excursion into post-*Bitches Brew* fusion, its knowledgeable appropriation of Indian and African elements more effective than Miles Davis' own. "Ticket to India", longer still, appeared on the CD reissue, a slacker performance but more revealing of Embryo's processes.

Nothing that followed was ever quite as confident or coherent. Burchard increasingly questioned the band's commercial direction, but his efforts to re-radicalise the group after the dull *Surfin'*, 1974, and *Bad Heads and Bad Cats*, 1975, failed to deliver another compelling recorded performance. Embryo became a travelling community, best caught on the road—which might mean anywhere from Egypt to Afghanistan, and in any atmosphere from archaeologically cool to politically urgent—or momentarily on *Apo Calypso*, which was recorded on the last day of 1976 with Gurtu and his mother Shobha Gurtu in the line-up. In retrospect, "Amnesty Total" plays like a throwing-over of static citizenship in favour of a dedication to exploration and movement. And so the Embryo story has run since. Arguably, its latter day incarnations are merely flags of convenience for Burchard's own activities rather than genuinely collective initiatives, but his vision and leadership have always been integral to the band and his contributions the key to the band's current concerns and the step about to be taken.

BM

Embryo in Casablanca. Courtesy Eurock Archives.

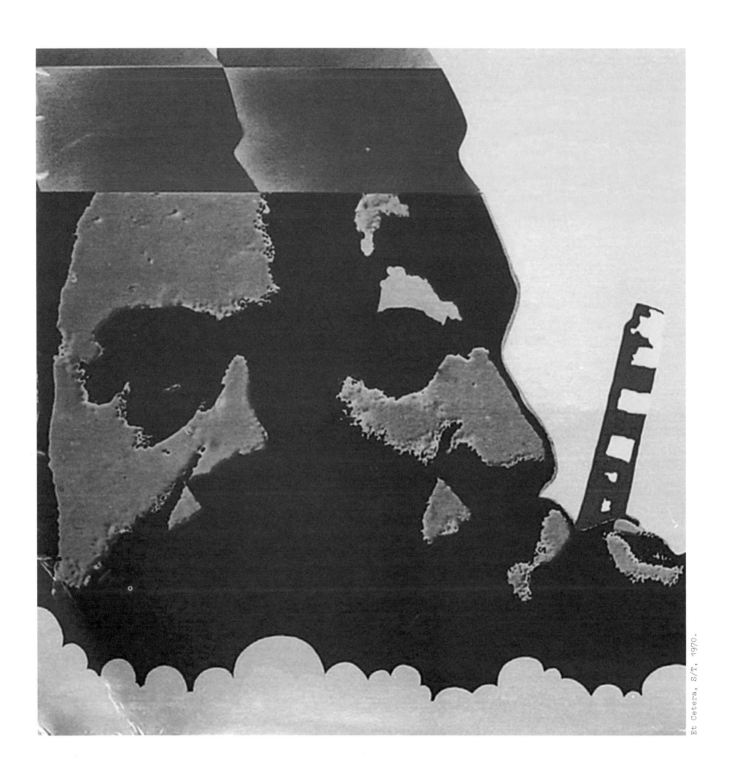

Et Cetera, S/T, 1970.

There can't have been many more successful rebrandings in music history than the 'formation' of Et Cetera. The group was essentially the jazz-oriented Wolfgang Dauner Quartet, renamed to catch the jazz-rock wave of the very late 1960s. Dauner was born in Stuttgart in 1935, a townsman and exact contemporary of composer Helmut Lachenmann. Dauner studied at the Musikhochschule—originally trumpet and composition—and gravitated towards the rising German jazz scene, gigging with saxophonist Joki Freund and others. He began recording under his own name in 1964, a trio date called *Dream Talk* with bassist Eberhard Weber and drummer Fred Braceful—also involved in the more ambitious *Free Action* two years later. *Dream Talk* traversed generic post-bop jazz, elements of Eric Dolphy's harmonic adventures on the signature "Sketch Up and Downer", and freer passages that made strong use of Jean-Luc Ponty's violin and Gerd Dudek's saxophones. Dauner continued to alternate between experimentalism and more straightforward jazz idiom, making a label debut for the still relatively young ECM with *Output* in 1970, an association that was not sustained, largely, one suspects, because Dauner was still dabbling in a variety of styles. In the same year, his quartet made the eclectic and strangely named *The Oimels*, which combined original and standard material with pop covers (Gershwin, 'Greensleeves', Lennon, McCartney), and saw Dauner moving in the direction of fusion. The release of *Et Cetera*, also in 1970, and the subsequent renaming of the group (not to be confused with the later Danish group Etcetera), allowed Dauner to reposition his music in jazz-rock while retaining an essentially jazz-based orientation. In their history of German music, *The Crack in the Cosmic Egg*, Steven and Alan Freeman even suggest that Dauner worked a subtle con, fudging his group's jazz background and adding a few psychedelic flourishes to what had been thoughtful and stretching modern jazz, which was then at a considerable market discount. Bonus tracks reissued with the CD of *Et Cetera* suggest how comfortably he assimilated jazz standards with a more rock-inflected programme.

Archive footage of Et Cetera suggests—not at all surprisingly—that the band's live performances remained more free flowing and improvisatory than the studio recordings suggest. A live date from Silmingen released in 1973 with a new group (Braceful remains, but Matthias Thurow is a lumpier bassist than Weber and flutist/vocalist Jürgen Schmidt Oehm lacks presence) is inferior to the original LP and the earlier group. With Siegfried Schwab on guitar, Weber creating additional lead lines on his cello, and Braceful combining heavy backbeats with Elvin Jones polyrhythms, the original album has considerable strengths. Like a great deal of German music at the time, 'ethnic' elements are given considerable prominence, with Arabic scales and cadences, trippy excursions that sound like modally-based raga form, episodes of free music that are closer to folk music practice than to free jazz. The 'poem' "Lady Blue" isn't a highpoint, but it does point to Dauner's considerable stylistic embrace and refusal to occupy a single creative pigeonhole.

Dauner's discography is strangely various, touching on the avant-garde, but also veering towards light jazz and easy listening on some of his MPS sessions. In later years, he was a key organising member of the multinational United Jazz + Rock Ensemble, and gradually returned to straight jazz playing with the likes of trombonist Albert Mangelsdorff and to a unique ethno-free approach with bandoneón player Dino Saluzzi and saxophonist Charlie Mariano. Perhaps the most musically literate and far-reaching German musician of his generation, Dauner is arguably only peripheral to the story of Krautrock, but he brought a unique intelligence to the form, and on the strength of *Et Cetera* and *Et Cetera* Live alone, he was among its most distinguished practitioners.
BM

ET CETERA/ WOLFGANG DAUNER

FAUST

The early 1970s were described by Uwe Nettelbeck as a "gold rush" period for the record industry, a time when money was speculatively lavished in all directions and a person like himself, connected with Polydor in Germany, could walk in and demand first class return tickets to New York on spec with no questions asked. It was in such financially abundant yet uncertain times that Faust were born. Nettelbeck, a journalist and Malcolm McLaren-esque figure, managed to persuade Polydor that he had in his hands a group with the potential to be the "new Beatles". They fused the nuclei of two previous groups, whose members included Jean-Hervé Peron, Werner "Zappi" Diermaier, Hans-Joachim Irmler, Rudi Sosna and Gunter Wüsthoff. On the basis of a demo tape and Nettelbeck's reputation as a 'tastemaker', Faust were not only signed to Polydor in 1970 but allowed access to a house and studio at Wümme, a former school just outside Hamburg, and given a year to work and play.

Listening to Faust now, and their anarchic, inebriated, disjointed sound collages sprayed with raw electronics and surging to crests of improvisational intensity, it is hard to think that, not once but twice in the 1970s, they were the carrier of high commercial hopes. They flailed gloriously in a zone between the extreme avant-garde and the James Last Orchestra. They named themselves Faust not only because of the kinetic energy implied in the German word for "fist" but also as a rueful allusion to their having sold their souls in signing to a major label. And yet, far from knuckling down in honest compromise, they not only recklessly squandered their time at Wümme on wine, woman dope and (only occasionally) song but eventually released a debut album which, while one of the key seismic events of Krautrock, was an unabashed commercial disaster area, biting off the hand that fed them.

Its opening could not have been more pointed—tapes of The Beatles' "All You Need Is Love" and The Rolling Stones' "Satisfaction" are symbolically set fire to in a blaze of electronics, crumpling and blackening before our ears. The assemblage that followed was quite new—'songs' like "Why Don't You Eat Carrots" and "Meadow Meal" were fragile, surreal, mock-banal affairs, buffeted by giant synthwaves. Holding it all together was brilliant engineer Kurt Graupner and his "black boxes", devices which, for example, enabled the group to play off manipulated and treated sounds in real time in the studio, adding a spontaneous element to the sonic contrivance. The second side was a primitive, jazz-rock jam, which then breaks off into what sounds like a drinking song before ending on an ectoplasmic treated organ motif.

For their second album, *So Far*, a pained Polydor demanded that they at least chop up their work into something resembling song form—they obliged, beginning with the almost sarcastically straight, pounding monotones of "It's A Rainy Day, Sunshine Girl". But this is eventually swept up into cirrus clouds of electronics and eventually rewards the listener with what Krautrock aficionado Julian Cope described as his favourite saxophone solo of all time. *So Far* was more structured but it still maintained all the characteristics of the group—an almost Dada-like, energetic juxtaposition of mock-MOR, noise and found elements, underpinned by a pastoral hankering for some lost unity, often epitomised in the delicate songwriting of the ill-fated Rudy Sosna.

It finally dawned upon Polydor that a million years of evolution might pass before Faust could be considered pop sensations and they were dropped. However, they immediately found a berth with Virgin Records in the UK, which yielded the albums *The Faust Tapes* (snippets of Faustania sold for an extraordinary low 50p in order to garner interest) and *Faust IV*, which contained the Faust-in-a-nutshell John Peel favourite "It's A Bit Of A Pain". But the group never really got along with Virgin head Richard Branson—on one occasion, he told them he was only paying them half of what they were due for a live concert and, in protest, Peron stripped down, saying that in that case, he would only wear half his clothes for the show. They found Virgin's Manor Studios, who had their own sound engineers, far less congenial than the detachment and absolute freedom of Wümme. Thereafter, Faust made some recordings in Munich—protracted, picaresque pieces eventually released on the album *Munic & Elsewhere* in which the group were like specks on their own, vast landscape, stretching into an unknown future.

Despite a revival in interest in the group following the reissue of their first two albums on Chris Cutler's Recommended Records label, which led to their being rediscovered by a whole new post-punk audience, Faust went to ground in the 1980s. Rudy Sosna sadly died and their only activities constituted rave-style parties in which they kept alive their collective pulse. However, in the early 1990s, they played what was initially announced as a one-off concert in London which proved so successful, with its use of onstage cement mixers and chainsaws that they decided to revive, releasing a series of albums, more fluid, drone-based and improvised in feel, held together by the percussive arsenal of "Zappi" Diermaier. They did a live soundtrack to the FW Murnau film *Nosferatu* and played the Royal Festival Hall alongside David Ball of Soft Cell, himself one who recognised Faust's role in using electronics to expand rock's lexicon. Faust have remained contemporary and active, even venturing into hip hop terrain with Dälek. However, in recent years, they have reverted once again to separate and, sadly, rival nuclei, with one version of "Faust" headed up by Jean-Hervé Peron and Zappi Diermaier, the other by Joachim Irmler. Still, for all their chaos and schisms, Faust are properly revered by those who take their Krautrock truly seriously. As Tim Gane of Stereolab remarked, when I interviewed him for an American magazine about Kraftwerk a few years ago, "to be honest, I wish we were talking about Faust".

DS

Courtesy Andy Wilson/faust-pages.com.

STEPHEN THROWER
ON FAUST

Faust, 1971, begins with a warm organic hum, from which a savage fuzztone escapes, flooding the synapses with electric intensity. A temporal-lobe assault—and a rush of pure endorphin. Within this ecstatic vortex, fragments of 'the classics' spin by— "I can't get no satisfaction"… "All you need is love"…

The uproar screeches to a halt. Cut to a frantic voice, urging obscure dissent against a cold classical piano figure. Cut again, to an ensemble performance, elliptical but achingly arty; some kind of effete oompah music. A combination of rock, chamber orchestra and bierkellar—trumpet, piano, bass, drums… and is that a harpsichord? Cut again, to a rock band blazing through a killer riff: trumpet in unison with heavily distorted guitar, feverish drums, and unison group vocals, like a drunken sing-song in a terrorist cell, or the Italian Futurists having a knees-up. Arcing above this exhilarating landscape is a synth—shrieking, antedeluvian and monstrous—sending power-shocks cascading from your scalp to your spasmodically clenching fingers and toes. The riff falls away to reveal a tape of two people conversing quietly in German (a post-coital chat, I used to think; in fact it's a discussion about turning vegetarian)…

From here, elements reoccur, relationships shift, sounds fade in and out. The album veers through agaric pastoralism and stormy weather; strident vocals insist "You are a fruit fork"; an improvised rock work-out is swamped by bizarre wah-wah guitar, and a croaking malevolent gargoyle hams up an operatic aria. By the end of the album your musical worldview has been ripped wide open.

Faust music appeared seemingly from nowhere. Now, looking back to 1971, the year of their debut album (aka "Faust Clear") there are a few precursors: The Beatles' experiments of course; The Velvets; the electronic jazz-rock savagery of King Crimson's 21st Century Schizoid Man; early Van Der Graaf Generator; Sun Ra's freeform keyboards. But the energy of Faust is different, the vibe more abstractly aggressive; a post-1968 'tearing up the plans' protest music, embracing randomness and placing violent juxtaposition at the heart of its musical agenda. The first album, and its next-but-one follow-up The Faust Tapes, owe as much to John Cage's theories of chance operations, or the cut-ups of William Burroughs and Brion Gysin, as they do to rock, or 'fusion'.

Faust in their 1970s incarnation were pretty much unknowable. Their album covers were pure artworks: playing with concepts of openness, and transparency (Faust, with its clear vinyl in a clear sleeve and X-Ray graphic); opacity and the hidden (So Far, swathed in Spinal Tap blackness concealing a portfolio of full colour artworks inside); access and inaccessibility (The Faust Tapes, an album sold for 50p, thus ensuring that the weirdest Faust music was also the most widely heard); or non-music and rejection of the classical (Faust IV, its cover striated with empty music staves). Not a single band photo adorned their first four albums (a 'refusal of identity' which San Francisco's The Residents developed further, by making a sardonic fetish of it).

"The rock group as total artwork" first gained currency in 1966 when The Velvet Underground allowed Andy Warhol to incorporate them into his Exploding Plastic Inevitable. Faust (like their British contemporaries and fellow collagists, the early Roxy Music) were disinclined to 'pay their dues' by gigging thanklessly on the established rock circuit, so in the autumn of 1971, with perhaps the Velvets and Warhol in mind, they opted—at the instigation of producer Uwe Nettelbeck—to stage a 'showcase' concert for an invited audience of industry insiders. It went catastrophically wrong: the complex electronic equipment was still being frantically soldered together as the audience waited, and the whole thing turned to farce, an Imploding Plastic Ineptitude which reportedly scarred some members for life whilst amusing others (Joachim Irmler calls it "the only true concert we ever did").

Faust were sometimes derided as a 'faux-rock' group—the gold standard of rock ethics being 'authenticity' (perfectly lampooned by Johnny Rotten's "we mean it, maaan" in "God Save the Queen"). Faust were constructed almost to order, the result of international record label Polydor asking music journalist Uwe Nettelbeck to find them "a German rock band that is any good". Bringing together a combination of anarchist musicians, Nettelbeck struck an unprecedented deal with Polydor, incorporating not just total artistic freedom for Faust but a stack of cutting edge equipment and their own recording studio into the bargain. 'Experimental' in a wraparound, 360 degree sense, Faust was a creative laboratory in which the 'guinea pigs' were also the technicians in charge. Tinkering around with sonic chemistry while conducting their own no doubt assiduous lysergical experiments, Faust was a car-crash of idealism into praxis: goodness knows what Polydor thought when they finally heard the results. (In the late 1960s / early 1970s, all kinds of freaks, chancers and acid-heads were getting their mitts on establishment money—think Dennis Hooper and his buddies, shooting vast amounts of film to deliver Easy Rider, a counterculture success the money-men could barely comprehend...)

Whereas Can, Faust's contemporaries in German rock, were fêted for their mystical qualities, Faust were militant absurdists, sarcastic anarcho-hippies—pranksters not Maguses. Less Gurdjieff, more Dada. The Faust trip could be blissful, or it could shatter into twitching fragments, but it felt totally irreligious.

And yet, as Alejandro Jodorowsky once said: "The universe is a comedy. The universe is the laugh of God." Laughter is everywhere in Faust, in the madness and the chaos, in the preposterous lyrics. It's there when they 'rock-out', and it hovers like a suppressed smirk during the prissy musicianship of their 'polite' moments. The smirk turns to a smile of pure pleasure on" I've Got My Car and My TV", which turns from artfully wonky consumer-satire to ecstatic riffing (and, as Julian Cope rightly said in his Krautrocksampler, one of the best sax solos ever). It's always a factor, this smile, full of wit and silliness and satire and the dizzy joy of nonsense. And the heavier the sound, the funnier it gets.

In Faust's music there's a delicious anarchy of volume, pitch, texture, speed, style, and audio quality. Punk, poor lame-duck punk, thought it had lightning in a bottle because its ambassadors 'couldn't play'. The punks said "never trust a hippy", but would you really trust someone who says he can't "play"?

Faust play, alright. Like mad, industrious children. They unplay. They antiplay. Beyond the artworks, beyond the artifice, there's always play—the pleasure and the freedom of it. Faust, for all their cleverness, their irony, their conceptualism, quite clearly LOVED making this music. You can hear it when things change and gel and agree; when things clash and burn and tear apart. Faust sound intensely, joyfully alive, revelling in sheer unrestricted creativity. Far from abstruse musical conceptualism, they play, brilliantly. They're the wildest children in Germany.

On September 6 1970, Jimi Hendrix left the stage for the last time. He was one of the featured acts at the Love-and-Peace Festival held on the Baltic island of Fehmarn. It was a bizarre occasion, with both Mungo Jerry and Peter Brötzmann on the bill. Hendrix actually played a day later than scheduled because torrential rain made the stage unsafe. He played his final gig to a mixture of boos and jeers, then made way for a satirical rock cabaret act from Köln. There were other Krautrock bands on the same bill, including Limbus 4 and Embryo, and while the occasion marked Hendrix's last ever live appearance, it was the first by Ton Steine Scherben (then still known as Rote Steine). The stage was unsafe; during their act, it burst into flames.

Some of this might be explained by the incendiary presence of the brilliantly named Floh de Cologne, straight on after the great guitar-burner and straight into a set that combined protest against the war in Vietnam with a series of savage assaults on corporate capitalism and the political puppetry of the mass media. Floh de Cologne

was formed as a political theatre group in January 1966, just days after Lyndon Johnson committed America to a continued presence in South East Asia until Communist aggression was reversed, pouring a further 8,000 troops into the theatre. The group was affiliated to the movement or principle of action known as *Außerparlamentarische Opposition* (Extra-Parliamentary Opposition) and the university-centred SDS, both of whom advocated new forms of protest and social action.

Almost a year before Woodstock, Floh de Cologne played at the Internationale Essener Songtage 1968, a politically inspired festival which included Frank Zappa among its board members. The group's origins in German political theatre were confirmed and consolidated by the more recent example of Zappa's Mothers of Invention and followed a similarly confrontational approach, leading to cancelled broadcast and performance contrast on vaguely articulated charges of obscenity, pornography and tendency to disrupt social order. Founding members Hansi Frank, Dieter Klemm, Markus Schmid, Gerd Wollschon and, more briefly, Britta

Courtesy Deutsches Kabarettarchiv Mainz.

Floh de Cologne

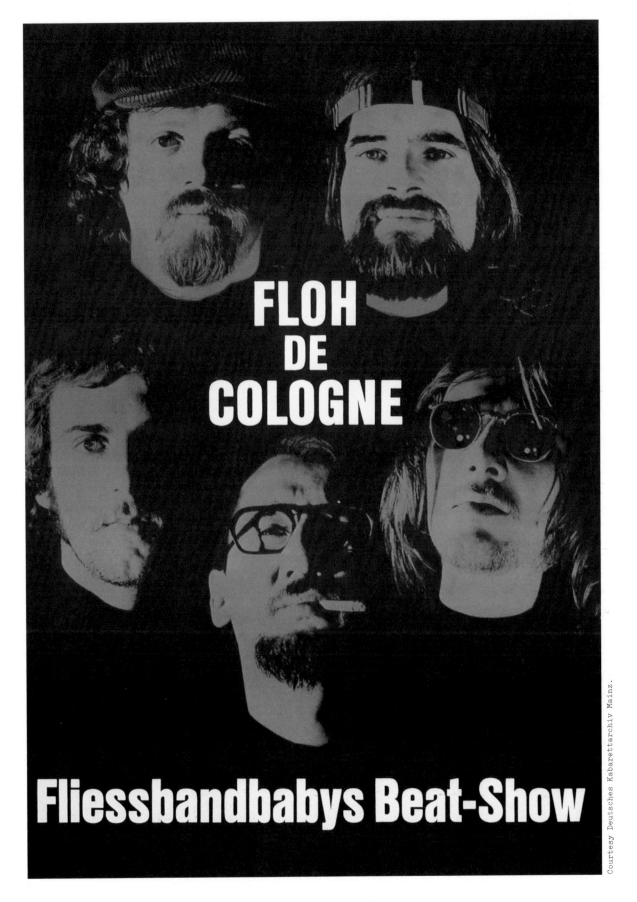

FLOH
DE
COLOGNE

Fliessbandbabys Beat-Show

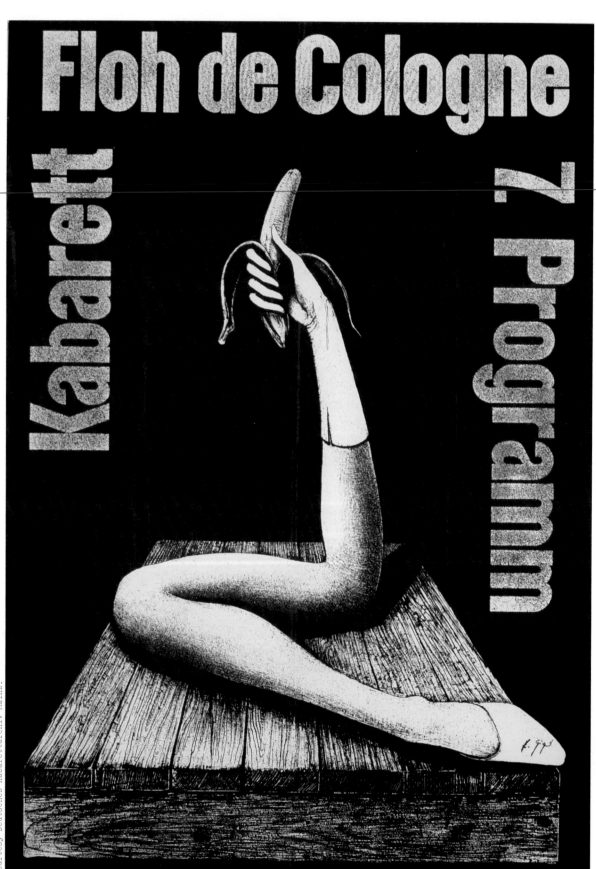

Baltruschat were supplemented by other instrumentalists and singer/speakers over what was a remarkably long lifespan for a satirical group. In later years, Floh de Cologne's style of protest and the records that resulted became increasingly commodified, but their earlier recordings like *Fliessbandbabys Beatshow*, *Rockoper Profitgier Live* and the ambitious *Geyer-Symphonie* (all released in Ohr, 1970–1973) didn't fail to launch attacks on the rock medium itself and its pretentious excesses.

The band's obsession with "profit vultures" (Gier/Geyer) meant that a difficult route had to be found between pop commerce and outfield resistance, and it is to Floh de Cologne's eternal credit that the line was held all the way till the farewell tour of 1983. During the later years, Floh de Cologne concentrated largely on multimedia presentation, calling in the talents of designer HR Giger and Wolfgang Niedecken. The visual impact of covers, posters and assorted multiples issued by the group was harsh but effective, often mitigating the group's sophomoric performance style which put substance ahead of presentation or style.

Floh de Cologne was a band of its moment that somehow managed to survive and transcend that moment and stand as a representative of rock music as perpetual opposition. Over perhaps half a dozen key albums—1975's *Tilt* is the last really important one—Floh de Cologne showed that the packaged LP medium was capable of delivering pungently contradictory messages about music business and its relationship to the wider culture. By embracing aspects of commercial culture, Floh de Cologne chipped at its foundations. The group has few distinctive progeny, testimony to its uniqueness but also to the courage of its satirical practice and lonely stance.

BM

Courtesy Deutsches Kabarettarchiv Mainz.

Like many of the original German bands, Gila was formed out of a group of political communards in Stuttgart. They began their musical existence as Gila Füchs in 1969. In tune with the spirit of those times, their original concerts combined free-form rock music with film, media, poetry and slide shows.

This period of experimental exploration led a couple of years later to the recording of their first album in a week's time at the studio of the famous producer Dieter Dierks. The band at that time was composed of Fritz Scheyhing (keyboards), Walter Wieder Kehr (bass), Daniel Alluno (percussion) and Wolfgang Conrad "Conny" Veit (guitar). The creative intent of the first album was to turn their instinct for musical aggression into a more free flowing intuitive form of communicating emotion via the medium of music. The band's name was shortened to simply Gila, and the album was nominally titled *Free Electric Sound*.

Released on BASF in the late summer of 1971, it certainly was a powerful example of those early psychedelic times. Both sides formed a heavy 'cosmic rock' collage full of swirling Hammond, Mellotron textures and Veit's acid guitar forays. It gained little notice at the time as BASF was not inclined to promote their early German rock releases. It wasn't until the original band had broken up and a second Gila album was released two years later that collectors discovered the first album and proclaimed it a great rarity. It then became valued as much for the fact

that it exchanged hands for a high price among German rock aficionados as for the excellent music it contained.

The second album, *Bury My Heart at Wounded Knee*, came out on Warner in late summer 1973. When the original Gila broke up, Conny Veit had gone on to play with Florian Fricke in Popol Vuh. The album's title was taken from a famous book about the US government's systematic genocide against the Native American people.

Musically it was totally different in style from the first band. Perhaps they kept Gila as the name instead of recording as Popol Vuh, due to the material's political associations, as conceptually Fricke/Popol Vuh were at the time highly devoted to the "sacred music" concept. The songs themselves were filled with majestic piano and Veit's magnificent electric/acoustic guitar playing, while vocals were nicely handled by Sabine Merbach. The music created by Florian and Connie along with Daniel Fichelscher (of Amon Düül II and Popol Vuh) was mantric and beautiful. In reality, that record was Gila in name only, as the music itself is most certainly in the vein of Popol Vuh.

The band did a bit of touring during the time of the second album's release and Conny Veit recorded again with Popol Vuh before going off to play with Guru Guru for a time. He then disappeared from the scene surfacing again only on some other recordings released later by Popol Vuh.

AP

Courtesy Garden of Delights.

The apex of higher-minded avant folk bliss, the holy grail of gone, Sergius Golowin's masterful 1972 LP *Lord Krishna Von Goloka* remains one of the major kosmische statements to come out of the whole Ash Ra/Klaus Schulze/Witthüser & Westrupp scene. Sergius Golowin was a modern polymath with a finger in a host of mutually exclusive disciplines: a green politician, an authority on folklore, tarot and mysticism, a friend of the Swiss Hell's Angels, a prodigious author, a model and confidante of the artist HR Giger… Journalist and visionary scenester Rolf-Ulrich Kaiser put Golowin together with a bunch of musicians that included Klaus Schulze, Bernd Witthüser and Walter Westrupp after encountering Golowin's treatise on herbs, witches and magic mushrooms, *Magie der Verbotenen Märchen* and realising he would make the perfect frontman for an instalment of his ongoing Cosmic Couriers psych rock series. The duo of Witthüser & Westrupp set the mood, with the kind of illuminated teutonic folk of their classic *Trips und Träume* LP but the addition of Klaus Schulze's heavenly keyboard raised the whole deal to another plane of there, with phantom choirs and drone ascensions set above chiming guitars and simple folk melodies. Golowin has a gone vocal style and his oracular descriptions of the blooming of flowers and the coming to of world consciousness are enough to make you want to split the scene and get naked in the white hills yourself. *Lord Krishna Von Goloka* was Golowin's sole LP but he was widely published in his lifetime, with his best known works in English being 1987's *The Gypsy Dreambook* and 1988's *The World Of Tarot*, the latter an elucidation of fellow Cosmic Courier Walter Wegmüller's Gypsy Tarot. Golowin passed away in 2006.
DK

Sergius Golowin and friend, 1972. Courtesy Eurock Archives.

SERGIUS GOLOWIN

GURU GURU

Few, if any, German groups in the late 1960s and early 1970s better represented the underlying idealism of the time than Guru Guru. Whereas some Krautrock groups were somewhat inward looking, hermetic, vague or even evasive when it came to the socio-political context in which they worked, Guru Guru explicitly made the connection between the radical music and the radical politics of their time, the student protests in particular. Their concerts were often punctuated with the reading of left-wing political statements and they considered the way in which they conducted themselves as a band to be 'political'. They lived communally (at one point inviting a group of native Americans to stay with them), braving brickbats for their long hair, and being dedicated to a mode of performance which they called "action music", designed to tease, challenge and jolt audiences out of their torpor and complacency. Drugs were practically a moral duty as well as a pleasure for the group. They would often take LSD before their gigs ("we wanted to get away from the A-B-A format in music as well as in our lives", they said), in order to add an element of unpredictability to affairs. They wore masks onstage or even introduced chickens into the proceedings, encouraging audiences to release their inner animal. All of this indirectly echoed the dadaist outrages of the early twentieth century, and so did an outdoor performance designed to ruin the peace of the entire city of Heidelberg—until the police shut them down.

Guru Guru have never ceased to operate but they have gone through at least 26 different line-ups in the course of their lifetime. As is often the case with commune-based German groups, however, there is one constant and dominant figure throughout. In the case of Guru Guru, it is their drummer and vocalist Mani Neumeier. Born in 1941 in Munich, he relocated in his teenage years to Zurich where he found work as a musician as early as 1959. In Switzerland, he also found himself more conveniently located to catch travelling jazzmen such as Louis Armstrong, Miles Davis, Thelonious Monk and John Coltrane, all of whom helped free up his musical sensibilities. By the mid-1960s he had joined the Irene Schweizer Trio and

had he kept his head down and concentrated on holding down the back seat, he could have carved out a more than respectable, even award-winning career in jazz. However, being part of the 'free' wing of the genre meant being alive to the free radicals in the air. He also worked with the Globe Unity Orchestra whose members (including Jaki Liebezeit, who later defected from jazz to join Can) were apt to mingle with the rock avant-garde.

And so, in 1968, Neumeier formed what was initially called the Guru Guru Groove Band with fellow jazz renegade Uli Trepte. For the first three years of the group's existence, they had no fixed abode, living aboard a tour bus on jam sandwiches and whatever else they could ingest. Thereafter, the shifting group membership lived communally in large houses, contributing to and taking from the household along Marxist lines.

They did not release their first album, *UFO*, until 1971 but a steady stream of releases has continued to this day. Guru Guru made no bones about their debt, or their nod to western music. They cited the likes of Jimi Hendrix, The Who and Frank Zappa in particular as influences, while their very name was an allusion to The Beatles' penchant for guru figures in the late 1960s. Hendrix is a particularly pronounced influence on tracks like "Oxymoron" from 1972's *Känguru*, although Neumeier's drumming buoys up the collective playing in great crests and surges. On "God's Endless Love For Men", meanwhile, from 1974's *Dance Of The Flames*, the tight, close-order playing is very reminiscent of The Mothers Of Invention during their own jazz-rock phase.

Neumeier and all those who have subsequently sailed in Guru Guru have maintained a steady course—listening to the 2005 studio album *In The Guru Lounge*, it's hard to find evidence of a group who have been buffeted amidships by modern developments. The 1970s style holds fast. However, Neumeier, who as well as leading Guru Guru has been involved in numerous collaborations, did involve himself in a techno project called Lover 303 which performed to some success in Goa in the late 1990s. Neumeier is modest about the provenance of Guru Guru's survival and continued audience; "perhaps it's something cosmic that goes through me and reaches the people", he speculated in 2002. Perhaps it is also to do with his own single-minded integrity and tirelessness.

DS

Courtesy Garden of Delights.

Harmonia. From left to right: Dieter Moebius, Hans-Joachim Roedelius, Michael Rother. Courtesy Moebius.

In 1971, Cluster's Dieter Moebius and Hans-Joachim Roedelius relocated to an intentional community at the village of Forst in Weserbergland, Lower Saxony. Here they sought refuge from the increasingly draining drug-and-alcohol-fuelled lifestyle of the urban avant-gardists.

Recognising a shared musical temperament, Michael Rother paid the duo a visit in April of 1973, hoping to recruit them as part of the NEU! live line-up for a planned UK tour. The plans never materialised but Rother, unhappy with the direction NEU! was taking, decided to join Cluster at Forst that summer, and so Harmonia was born.

"The name Harmonia (harmony)" says Rother "was an expression of our goal but also a small joke because, being very different personalities and coming from different backgrounds, we struggled over the music straightaway. We also discovered a pennant in our cellar that read 'Harmonia Ottenstein' (Ottenstein being a small town nearby)."

Life at Forst was as much about cooking, strolling and chopping wood as it was about music, and the trio discussed the potential of a new sound, one that would take the Cluster hallmarks of unearthliness and improvisation and meld them into something that was, well, pop music, at least compared to anything heard from Cluster thus far.

The first result was 1974's *Musik Von Harmonia*, with its daft cover depicting a colossal bottle of detergent. Two tracks were recorded live, "Sehr Kosmisch" at Paradiso in Amsterdam and "Ohrwurm" during their first performance in Forst, and the album was mixed and recorded by the band. Opening track "Watussi", set the tone with Roedelius' relentless contra-rotating melodies played out against tidal guitar drones and Moebius' controlled detonations of electronic scatter, all layered over Rother's primitive, stomping drum machine rhythms. The album presented a beautiful, alien world awash with colours and sounds unseen and unheard on our own planet, appropriate for the Forst landscape which features regularly in the tales of the Brothers Grimm. Breezes blow inverted rainbows across azure leaves, dark shapes glide through cyan shimmering waters while maddening rubber melodies flow over it all like swarming caterpillars. Later, on

HARMONIA

"Ahoi!", a track that appears to have made a lasting impression on future collaborator Brian Eno, a delicate stillness takes hold, shaped only by gently plucked guitars and distant organ swells. Recorded at Forst, *Musik Von Harmonia* remains fresh, exciting and extremely odd, with a strange, laidback charm that is rarely matched by today's clean and quantised electronicists.

A recently unearthed live recording of Harmonia in 1974 captures a more unruly, though no less engaging, picture of the band; Rother solos his way into the stratosphere over the unending crunch and thud of drum machines and ever-spinning organ ditties. It was at about this time that Brian Eno would seek out the trio, having been deeply impressed with their debut album, joining them for a jam in a 1974 concert in Fabrik, Hamburg.

Having completed contractual duties with the ever-troubled NEU!, Rother returned to Forst and, as Harmonia, the team produced another miracle of an album, 1975's

Deluxe, co-produced by Conny Plank. *Deluxe* was recorded on Plank's mobile 16-track equipment in Forst in June 1975 and mixed at his Cologne studio the following month. After the DIY-kronkiness of *Musik Von Harmonia* and Cluster's *Zuckerzeit* (which, contrary to the back sleeve credit, was not co-produced by Rother), the sheer majesty of *Deluxe* is astounding. If those first albums are gingerbread houses then *Deluxe* is a country manor, but one that is infinitely larger on the inside than it could ever be on the outside. The eponymous nine-minute opening track alone rages with incandescent, cosmic glory while still sounding like a goofily anthemic German drinking song. "Walky Talky" brings Guru Guru's wildman drummer Mani Neumauer into the mix for a rolling surfboard ride through the ionosphere, and then they pull off seven minutes of absurd parallel universe stadium rock with "Monza" before touching down gently three tracks later with the lilting, frogs'n'ivories closer "Kekse".

Harmonia, 1975. Courtesy Michael Rother. Photo: Ann Weitz.

Harmonia came to an end in the early summer of 1976, all three members immediately continuing with their individual projects, but the line-up returned in September of the same year for a final recording session with Brian Eno, who was on his way to Montreux to work on David Bowie's *Low*. "Eno" Rother recalls, "was very pleasant and inquisitive. We worked as equal partners and were a collective that simply wanted to make music, without the pressures of having to record an album and with no thoughts of commercial success". It was two decades before the recordings become available, partly because Eno's original tapes were considered lost and partly because the sessions were never intended for commercial release. However, Rother and Roedelius had made copies of the four track tapes and, in 1997, the recordings saw the light of day under the title *Harmonia 76: Tracks and Traces*. The album, which includes the chuggingly intense motorik "Vamos Campaneros" and the synth-and-guitar-at-play field recordings of "By the Riverside", still exudes a calm, unearthly beauty that sets it far apart from the increasingly bombastic direction that so much experimental rock music was moving in at the time.

The 1997 release had, in its atmospheric emphasis, a definite Roedelius feel; in fact, due to disagreements with the band, Roedelius remastered the material in his possession without the help of either Rother or Moebius, although both approve of the final result ("Möbi and I weren't happy that Achim went it alone, but we had to admit that he had done a hell of a job" says Rother). A 2009 reissue of *Tracks and Traces* released under the name "Harmonia and Eno 76" includes three additional songs that Rother unearthed, edited and mastered from his own archives.

After the '76 sessions, life took the trio onto divergent paths. Cluster recorded a couple more albums while, after the collapse of NEU!, Rother pursued a very successful solo career. Then, in late 2007, after 31 years of absence, Harmonia— Moebius, Roedelius and Rother—reformed for a series of successful performances around Europe, US and Australia, a reformation that ended in 2009. No future releases are planned beyond a reissue of *Tracks and Traces*.

Even within the wildly unpredictable Krautrock universe, and the narrow social confines of the music scene of the time, Harmonia (and their zygote group Cluster) were just, well, different. Says Rother: "Even though I respected Kraftwerk and Can, I wanted my music to be different from what they did. I wasn't impressed by what happened in Berlin or Munich at the time. Any box or label that is attached to our music tries to neglect the fact that we weren't a 'family' of German musicians, we had no common goals or identity." Adds Roedelius: "we didn't fit into the category Krautrock at all, because we weren't part of it, even though it was said that we were. We didn't care, we belonged to the arts scene as well as to the popular music scene."

MP

Michael Rother in Harmonia's studio, 1973. Photo: Ann Weitz.

KRAFTWERK

Like many groups in the Krautrock era, it is only during the lengthy period of time since they have, by and large, ceased operating, that Kraftwerk's achievements have been properly appreciated. They first attained international notoriety with *Autobahn*, from which the single of the same name is culled. This was 1975, the year when the UK rocked with uneasy laughter at John Cleese goosestepping up and down the corridors in Fawlty Towers; the year when the quartet leered benignly into the cameras of Tomorrow's World, and when Lester Bangs, then the doyen of American rock journalists, asked them if their new robotic sounds represented a "final solution" for music. Few could get past their "Germanness" and the perverse novelty of eschewing guitars in favour of electronics. Fewer still realised that they were quietly laying the cables that would underpin not just the rock music of tomorrow, but also electrify funk and dance.

Kraftwerk were formed around 1970, by Ralf Hütter and Florian Schneider, both of whom started out as Düsseldorf Conservatory students, and came from well-heeled West German middle class backgrounds. "We had no fathers", Hütter once said, speaking metaphorically. Initially, the Hütter/Schneider nucleus went under the name of Organisation, but despite the formalist overtones of that moniker and the rhythmical emphasis of their first and only album *Tone Float*, there appeared little to distinguish this album from the amorphous, aromatic swirl of oriental-tinged trance-rock in vogue in Germany at the turn of the decade.

So informal were the shifting line-ups of Kraftwerk that, temporarily, Ralf Hütter was not even part of the group in the early 1970s, dropping out between their first and second albums. These were a mixture of agitated flute solos, wobbly varispeed electronics and brief, tentative attempts to apply the ideas of Stockhausen in a rock context ("Atem", for example). Their early 1970s albums have a relatively unspoiled and unplundered feel about them, with tracks like the nowadays relatively unfamiliar "Ananas Symphonie" from *Ralf & Florian* idyllically melding the organic and the synthetic in a manner that reminds (pre-minds?) of The Orb.

However, it was with 1975's *Autobahn* that the smoke around Kraftwerk really

Kraftwerk, from left to right: Florian Schneider, Ralf Hütter, Karl Bardos, Wolfgang Flür. Courtesy Eurock Archives.

clears, with the group revealing themselves in all their deceptively pellucid serenity. The main, title track is a glistening, beautifully realised tone poem to automobile travel, from ignition to pulling out the driveway, to bowling along sunlit grey lines to weaving through heavy traffic, to the gentle swerve of the carriageway towards a final destination. It's a sonic transcription, which suggests, quite at odds with the agrarian tendencies of the counterculture of the day, that the relationship between man and machine can be an untroubled one. This was the theme of their notorious interview with Lester Bangs the same year. As Ralf Hütter said, "It's like a robot thing, when it gets up to a certain stage. It starts playing...it's no longer you and I, it's It." That the Autobahns had been inaugurated by Hitler, however, marked Kraftwerk out as reactionaries—something they played up to, as provocateurs, in the Bangs interview, casually alluding, for example, to the "German mentality, which is more advanced". Fellow Germans, furthermore, sporting their "Atomkraft? Nein, Danke" ("Nuclear power? No

thanks") badges, were indignant at what they took to be Kraftwerk's endorsement of nuclear power on their next album *Radioactivity*.

1977's *Trans-Europe Express* is, for many, Kraftwerk's supreme statement. Posing in suits in idyllic, Germanic settings like colorised postcards, the album is ostensibly triumphant once more about man's harmonious working relationship with technology but, in its own, deadpan way allows for some existential reflection on tracks like "Showroom Dummies" and "The Hall Of Mirrors". Furthermore, the title track rises to an uneasily brutal crescendo, with faint inklings of *La Bête Humaine*. *Trans-Europe Express* isn't so much about futurism as making links between past and present (as in the track "Franz Schubert") and the landscape of "elegance and decadence" noted on "Europe Endless". It's about reconnecting with old German traditions, back to Weimar and the great composers, tunnelling through the historical irruption of the Third Reich.

David Bowie had been among the first to turn onto Kraftwerk with *Trans-Europe Express*. By the time of 1978's *The Man*

Machine and 1981's *Computer World*, however, a new and prolific era of synthpop was dawning, in which the possibilities of Krafwerk's smart, economical, sequencer-driven style was greeted as a perfect model in a post-punk era in which longhair and guitar excess was being ruthlessly sheared back. Despite disappearing for three years to work, in part, on the live act which has provided a working basis for their onstage appearances ever since, Kraftwerk were not just à la mode at this time but acting as clear harbingers for the future. 1978's "The Model" was a retrospective number one hit in 1982. Around this time, Afrika Bambaata used the electronic undergirding of the track "Trans-Europe Express" as the basis for his "Planet Rock", thereby inaugurating electro-funk, whose ramifications in the world of African-American music, from techno to hip-hop, would be huge and long-lasting.

However, in the era of Gary Numan, Human League, Depeche Mode, Soft Cell, etc, all of whom carried the Kraftwerkian spoor into the 1980s and beyond, Kraftwerk themselves began to recede. In 1983, they released the 12" "Tour De France", a vivid homage to the motion of the bicycle chain (they were keen cyclists) and in 1986 the album *Electric Cafe*, which mooted a "Techno-Pop" that was, in truth, already very much in existence. Their work was done. Since then, a few remixes and a short piece for "Expo 2000" apart, they have kept a very low profile, re-emerging occasionally onto the live circuit but locked away in the secrecy of their Kling Klang compound. Old members have left, most notably Florian Schneider in 2008, new members been added. When Karl Bartos wrote a memoir in which he tried to lift the lid on the group's supposed backstage peccadilloes, they tried to suppress it, but understandably so. Whereas other groups trade on their uproarious past, Kraftwerk's aim is complete self-effacement. After all, they have always been provocatively antithetical to traditional rock values—effete (posing on rouge on the cover to *The Man Machine*) not macho, emotionally understated rather than overwrought, synthetic rather than "authentic", Germanic rather than Anglo-American, besuited rather than bejeaned, in harmony with the modern world rather than dramatically at odds with it. One by one they have successfully stood in implied opposition to rock's values and hoary taboos, and in so doing, helped rock evolve. Who doesn't pay them homage nowadays?

DS

Kraftwerk live at Sydney Capitol Theatre, 1981. Photo: Bob King.

La Düsseldorf in 1974. Courtesy Miki Yui. Photo: Sabine Critall.

La Düsseldorf are sometimes considered one of the footnotes of Krautrock history, yet David Bowie went so far as to describe their music, in advance, as "the soundtrack to the Eighties". Certainly, in its sleek, urbane yet high octane and motorik way, it gives a sense of what an 1980s might have been like had punk not dynamited everything in the late 1970s: compact, serene, progressive, mechanically elegant and evolved.

La Düsseldorf were formed by Klaus Dinger, formerly drummer of NEU!, and also included his brother Thomas, who took care of percussion while Klaus tried his hand on guitar. The third member of the group was Hans Lampe, on electronics. Despite all musical appearances, the relationship between NEU!'s Michael Rother and Klaus Dinger had always been a fractious one, and despite having achieved an artistic apex with their 1975 album *NEU!75*, the querulousness between the pair rent them asunder. Dinger had always been more inclined towards noise and exuberance than the ambient melodicism favoured by Rother. This had created an exquisite, paradoxical tension which made NEU! the band they were. However, that duality persists, to some extent, in La Düsseldorf. Their first, eponymous album, released in 1976, opens with "Düsseldorf", which glides along over 13 delicious but untroubled minutes, generating exhaust fumes of endorphins. Dinger, however, cannot resist breaking into silly, operatic vocals and there is a self-mocking facetiousness in the lyric, which consists of the word "Düsseldorf" repeated, over and over.

"La Düsseldorf", which follows, is an uncanny anticipation of punk mores. Over a spitfire rhythm, Dinger now chants the word "Düsseldorf" with an almost Johnny Rotten-like edge, over guitars and keyboards travelling in skinny, straight white lines. The track opens with a sampled passage of chanting at a sports event, which might have seemed like a real farewell to 1970s prog—except that the same device is used by Pink Floyd on their album *Meddle*. The remainder of the album is a sophisticated balance of the monochrome and the colourised, as if surveying the landscape of the coming decade from a mountaintop of anticipation, an imaginary Europe endless. "Silver Cloud", taken from this album, became a deserving if unlikely hit single.

By 1978, however, there were emerging signs that things were panning out along different lines. La Düsseldorf now found the terrain they'd been used to having largely to themselves crowded out by aspiring electropop usurpers. They were perfectly placed to take advantage of this, which accounts for the relatively high album sales they enjoyed in their lifetime. The opening, title track of their second album *Viva* is almost a triumphal stomp, with Klaus Dinger once again exhibiting his predilection for raucous, almost intoxicated, bierkeller vocals. However, the metal abstractions of a track like "Rheinita" showed that as well as looking forward, La Düsseldorf had a retrospective awareness of an experimental legacy, even as the punk/post punk party raged around them. "Cha Cha 2000" concludes, however, with Dinger once again sounding convivial, like a man on top of things, on top of the world, arms round the shoulders of his comrades.

In 1981, La Düsseldorf released their third and final album *Individuellos*, initially in Germany alone. Again, it's the sound of a group who have long since progressed to, and arrived at the place they want to be. However, by now, Klaus Dinger's exuberant vocal contributions are beginning to grate a little, and, while these synth-based song structures stand up to any amount of kicking of the tyres, there is a growing sense that here is a band who have said all they needed to say. It has some bracing moments, for sure, particularly "Lieber Honig 1981", with its off kilter, church hall piano and ragged, Spectoresque reverb. However, in a pop world now replete with everyone from OMD and Depeche Mode to Soft Cell, La Düsseldorf, for all their best efforts, no longer sounded so distinctive. In Germany, too, there was a new wave (the "Neue Deutsche Welle"), spearheaded by the likes of DAF and Der Plan, all of whom owed a debt to the preceding generation but who brought a fresh rubrix of ideas all their own.

Wisely, La Düsseldorf wound up at this point, still at a relative high. Klaus Dinger did, however, issue two albums under his own name, *Néondian* in 1985 and *Die Engel des Herrn* in 1993. His last unfinished project before his death was called la-Duesseldorf.de, and two albums of related material—*VIVA RIMIX* and *Japandorf.com*—will be released in 2010. Dinger died in 2008. **DS**

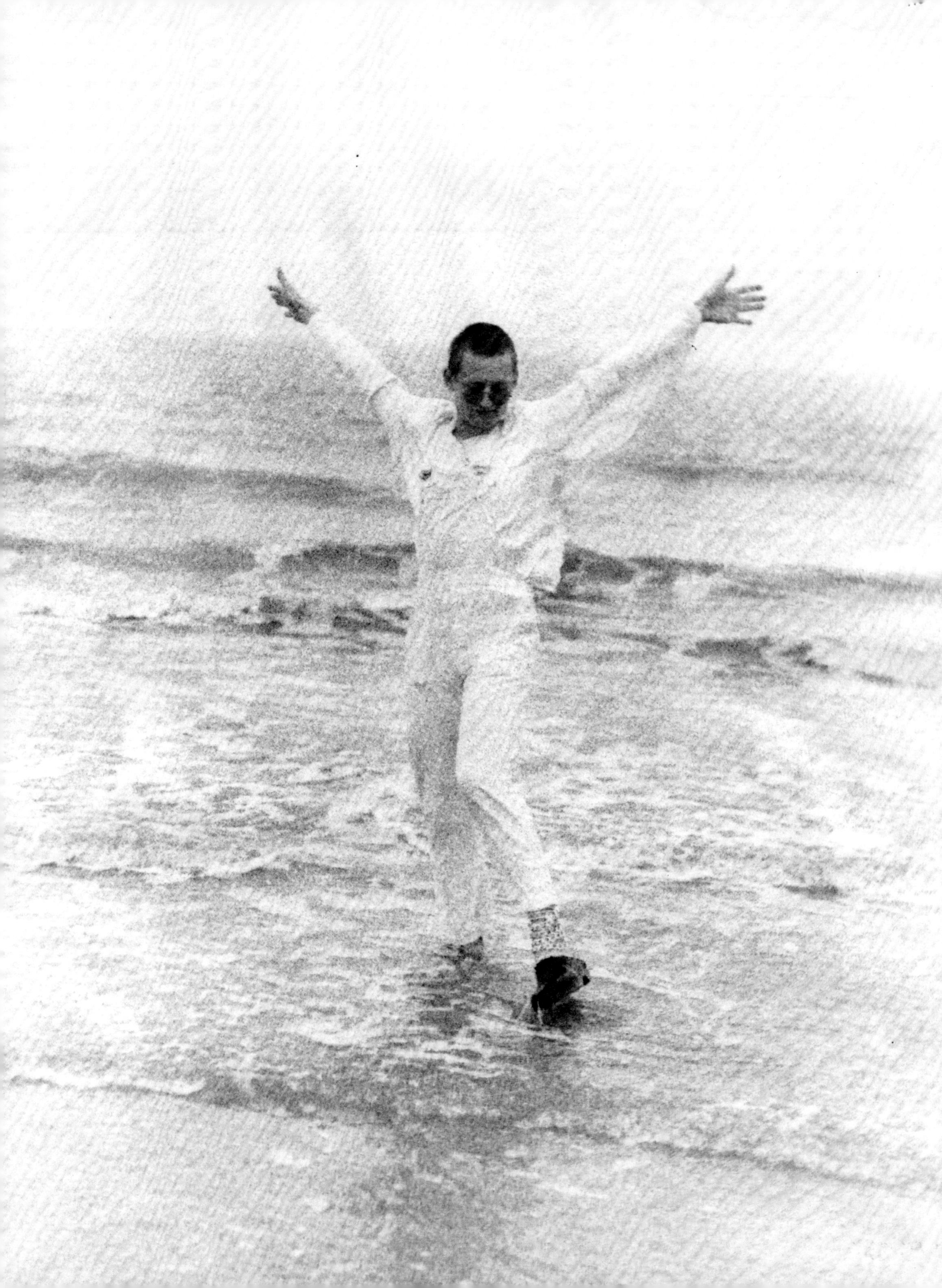

Klaus Dinger. Courtesy Miki Yui.

Klaus Dinger in 1969. Courtesy Miki Yui.

STEPHEN THROWER
ON LA DÜSSELDORF

Bright, effervescent, buoyant, infectious. Not words that necessarily spring to mind when Krautrock is discussed, but fine words to describe what I love about La Düsseldorf. Back in the early days of punk I was attracted first by the sleeve of their debut LP, with its inky-blue night-time cityscape and graffiti-ish writing. Wrapped inside were simple song structures, relentless rhythms and bar chord guitars, all of which echoed the punk ethos—but the candy-coated melodiousness of the music was hardly what I was expecting. The album pulses and glows, ramping up the "fun fun fun" of Kraftwerk's "Autobahn" into sheer sensual enjoyment. Listening to it, you feel like a dog with its head out the window of a fast-moving car, lapping up pure sensation.

The second album, *Viva* (1978), is a neglected masterpiece. In places, the opalescent eurosynths and pounding piano remind me of Abba circa 1979. It's an album so obscenely warm and cheerful that it makes the contemporary synth hits of Jean Michel Jarre sound like extracts from Throbbing Gristle's *2nd Annual Report*.

I was initially put off by reviews of *Individuellos*, the third album. It's frequently dismissed as a watered down disappointment, and considering how feather-light the other two are, how unappetising does that sound? However, years later when I got around to listening I realised that it's easily as good as *Viva*, and it actually has a streak of experimentalism that takes it further out than the other two. Great lyrics ("No von likes me, und no von likes you" shouts Dinger cheerily), two tracks without drums (shocking!), and a song featuring someone imitating horse-hooves with their tongue—brilliant childlike inspiration.

I've always found the sheer unabashed cheeriness of the group a pleasing enigma. Were they reacting to the other major players in the Krautrock scene? Or were they simply doing their own thing, devoid of the need to challenge anything? Whatever the reason for this ecstatic, silly, boisterous music, we should all give thanks to the memory of Klaus and Thomas Dinger, who surely intended to wipe the floor with heavy trips and deliver us from all headfuckery!

R.I.P. Klaus Dinger (March 30, 1946—March 21, 2008)
R.I.P. Thomas Dinger (October 28, 1952—April 9, 2002)

Limbus' name is either an archaic variant on Limbo (a realm now no longer recognised by the Catholic Church), a poetic word for prison, a border or fringe in biology or botany, or else a technical term for the rim or lip of a volcanic crater. It hardly needs a second guess to decide which is most appropriate for the group comprised of Odysseus Artnern, Bernd Henninger and Gerd Kraus, who play a specified but undifferentiated instrumentarium on some of the darkest and most probing music in the Krautrock canon. Lent additional cachet and mystery by appearing on the infamous Nurse with Wound List of esoteric influences, the group occupies only a shadowy position in the hinterland of most contemporary music fans.

Established in Heidelberg in 1968, the group vented a pungent magma of free improvisation and ethnic elements, strikingly different from Christian Burchard's more commercially oriented experiments with Embryo. Limbus offered a "Cosmic Music Experience", subtitle of the rare and obscure *New Atlantis* LP that emerged in 1969. In its egoless and non-idiomatic approach to canonical instruments—violin, piano—the music is remarkably similar in spirit, though not in basic sonority, to that of British improvisers (and fellow Nurse with Wound-listers) AMM. Randomly distributed folk elements mean that the comparison is limited, though.

Never captive to any kind of generic expectation, Limbus made no move toward the mainstream. The group's second LP *Mandalas*, released in 1970, was also the second release on the influential Ohr label. By this point, with the addition of Matthias Kniepper, it had become Limbus 4. The philosophy was ostensibly the same, but there was a new richness of colouration in the music, and less dependence on real-time improvisation and more on studio layering and tessellations, giving the album an intriguing air of contrivance that is at odds with the free-flowing spontaneity of much German progressive music of the period.

One acute observer/listener likens Limbus 4's soundscapes—"Kundalin", "Dhaniya", "Plasma"—to the "ethnological forgeries" spoken of by Can, and spoken of without reproach. These tracks sound like field recordings from the edge, unexpectedly crisp documentation of 'ethnic' materials whose purpose cannot be guessed, or can only be guessed. The titles are arguably too specific and associative for music as fugitive as this, and *Mandalas* is best heard without reference to the track listings or the instrumental credits. There are kazoos in there, or something very like them, and sounds which can only have been created by a series of directed accidents. Its power lies in its inability to suggest any of the familiar cultural hegemonies. This isn't 'western' music, and nor is it 'eastern' or 'African'. It is the music of the Preterite, or permanently overlooked.

BM

English rock quartet achieves chart success with a rock 'opera' about a blind kid: it couldn't happen, or at least it couldn't happen twice, surely? Against all odds, it did. Four years after Pete Townshend's genre-shifting Tommy for the Who, and at a time when Steven Spielberg was still a tyro director, Nektar bounced into the US top 20 with *Remember the Future*, a concept album about a sightless boy who communicates with an extraterrestrial being.

Nektar had already followed on the heels of another English group. The band's four members—guitarist Roye Albrighton, keyboardist Allan "Taff" Freeman, bassist Derek "Mo" Moore and drummer Ron Howden—had all come to Hamburg with other groups, all of them trying to capture the same musical magic as the Beatles had a few years earlier. They individually gravitated to the Star Club where they met and the idea of Nektar took shape. The debut album appeared on Bellaphon two years later in 1971. *Journey to the Centre of the Eye* is conventional, inner-space stuff, tracked by a weighty prog sound. Live performances were enhanced by 'fifth member' Mick Brockett's liquid lights and Keith Walters' slides. "The Nine Lifeless Daughters of the Sun" was typical: so many! so lifeless! The sequels, *A Tab in the Ocean* and *...Sounds Like This* were better. The former's long title track established the group's trademark idiom: slow variation of relatively simple material in a style that echoed the bombast of Emerson, Lake & Palmer and anticipated the hypnotic slippages of the Necks.

At about the same time as the song-based *...Sounds Like This*, Nektar recorded *Remember the Future*, just two long LP-side tracks.

The record was the group's first American release and Nektar made its American live debut at the Academy of Music in the autumn of 1974, using such a range of equipment and amplification that all power to the building was fused. *Down to Earth*, 1974, was another concept album, this time a circus story, but despite—or perhaps because of—a large guest cast that included 'ringmaster' Robert Calvert, singer PP Arnold and trombonist Chris Pyne, it lacked the brazen impact of its predecessor.

Nektar returned to songs with *Recycled* in 1975, the group's most effective record musically, rhythmically astute and with a wry edge that reminded listeners that the members' background was pastoral-English rather than industrial-Kraut. The CD release of Nektar's best album was a disaster; the wrong mix was used and Albrighton was inaudible. The oversight retrospectively anticipated his departure from the group, replaced by Dave Nelson before the dreary *Magic Is a Child* in 1976. It has its admirers but most non-specialists only know it because the 11-year old, pre-Vogue Brooke Shields is on the cover, emerging from a waterfall. Albrighton was back for *Man in the Moon* in 1980, but it was to be a curtain call, a shadow of *Remember the Future*. The group's creative energies seemed increasingly dissipated across genres: prog, psychedelia, heavy rock, r'n'b, and without the ability to improvise effectively at some length its material seemed increasingly insubstantial. Though there was to be a reunion in 2001, it was to be live tapes of *Remember the Future* gigs that would sustain the fans in the years ahead.

BM

Michael Rother (left) and Klaus Dinger (right) on Dinger's bed, 1971. Courtesy Miki Yui. Photo: Thomas Dinger.

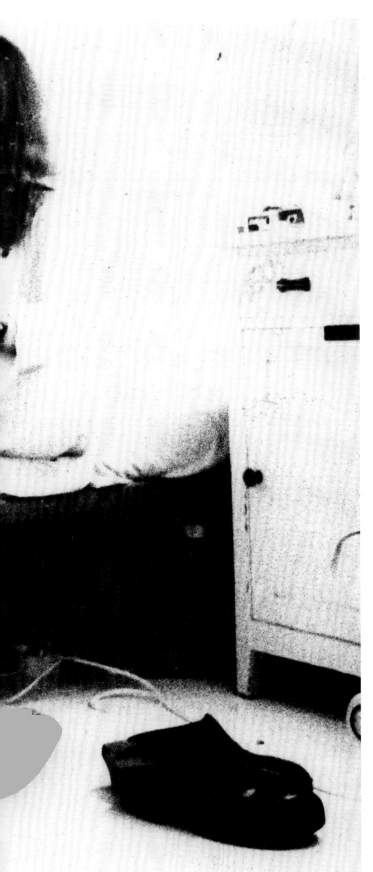

NEU!: always written in block capitals and with an exclamation mark: a pop art slogan.

It's like breaking the pain barrier. After a few minutes, boredom sets in—when are they going to get to the chorus? Suddenly, something clicks. It's about the journey, not the destination. There isn't going to be a chorus, a middle 8 or a sugary sax solo. This is it—a fantastic, danceable beat, glorious sounds, a pulsing propulsion in the purest, ego-free expression of joy. An intense, visceral, physical experience: a trip. This is the epiphany of getting NEU! After that, traditional song structure feels… normal. Redundant.

Düsseldorf, 1971. There came a realisation amongst many artists that German youth needed to recreate itself—to distance itself from their recent history and to invent a future. Michael Rother, a noted young guitarist in the Düsseldorf scene who in 1965 had started playing pop music by copying UK beat bands, realised that he had to leave the heroes of his early days behind, and decided to forge his own musical identity.

Klaus Dinger, a 'total' artist and drummer who rallied against the idea that "you could just buy good taste", lived in a Düsseldorf commune, painted completely white—the word "Neu!" was everywhere. Dinger and Rother first worked together in Kraftwerk, touring Germany and making two television appearances. Whilst recording Kraftwerk's second album, the band—Florian Schneider, Dinger and Rother—began to feel dissatisfied with the recordings, and so Dinger and Rother quit to form NEU! They had already decided that Kraftwerk's producer, Konrad "Conny" Plank, was the man for the job.

Plank, a former sound engineer at West Deutsche Rundfunk, was fascinated by the possibilities of new technology such as rhythm boxes. He was the man responsible for producing Harmonia, Cluster, Kraftwerk, and many other Krautrock bands. His work with NEU! in particular tested his skills as a collaborator as much as an engineer. His idea for mixing was "Alles verbiegen und verkurbeln!" (Turn everything upside down and inside out!).

Dinger, an extrovert "wild on LSD" (in his own words] vied with Michael Rother: the calmer, more considered half of the band.

NEU! live, 1972. Courtesy Miki Yui.

16.11.72
NEU!

NEU! [aka *NEU!1*] was recorded in four days in December 1971 on 8-track in Hamburg, Germany and released in 1972 by Brain Records. It was pure Krautrock: it was studio-as-instrument, studio-as-band, pop art, a Pandora's box of pneumatic drills, an angry crowd, a terrifying wall of knife-edge guitars, motorik abandon, Rother's glistening, inimitable, transcendental "dehgitarre", sudden dives into soundpools of processed cymbal sounds and eerie electronic feedback. It was exhilarating yet praeternaturally calm at the same time. Proud, authentic, uncompromisingly repetitive, it was unrelenting in its joy, in its eagerness to take you in its streamlined machine down the Autobahn.

Michael Rother: "that was what made NEU!—the idea of fast-forward movement—of an endless flight, with our eyes focused upon the horizon." NEU! musik. Deconstructed rock, reduced to its core elements, stripped to its purest essence; Rother's uncluttered rhythmic hypnosis, Dinger's disciplined, powerful drumming. The motorik beat: meant to be a portmanteau combining the German words "motor" and "musik", it means nothing in German, but does convey continuous forward motion. Described by Brian Eno as one of the "three great beats of the '70s", Dinger [every inch the rock god—flowing hair, glitter suit, shades—most notably in Kraftwerk's "Ruckstoss Gondolero" on their Beat Club appearance] said: "I have never called the beat 'the motorik' myself. That sounds more like a machine and it was very much a human beat. Instead I called it 'lange Gerade' or 'endlose Gerade', or 'Apache'. It's a feeling, like a picture, like driving down a long road or lane. It is essentially about life, how you have to keep moving, get on and stay in motion."

It was a human beat, inspired by a human devotion: "Lieber honig" was a Swedish girl, Anita. Her businessman father disapproved of her relationship with Dinger and so moved the family to Norway, which eventually split them up. "Hero" [on *NEU!75*] begins with Dinger shouting "back to Norway!". She appears in song, inspiration and in recording on: "Im Glück", "Lieber Honig" and "Gedenkminute (für A + K)".

It was a human beat: but it wasn't all beats: the focus was also timbral change around processed guitar, spatialisation; from the palliative "Weissensee" to "Lieber Honig", featuring stoner vocals by Dinger, leading out into the lock-groove at the end of the vinyl version. For 1971, this was extraordinary…

Confident in their invention of something genuinely new, they "…walked against the wall and just walked through" [Rother], into the experimental world of *NEU!2*: recorded in February 1973.

Michael Rother said in an interview with the Kosmische Show that they realised they had created something special with "Hallogallo" [from *NEU!1*)—"the frailty of 'Hallogallo' is something that is connected to the beauty and to the magic"—and wanted to recreate it. At 11 mins 14 secs "Für Immer" [Forever] blasts its way into the centre of your soul and throbs and pulses gloriously using just one chord, not once losing its firepower, direction or intensity.

"Super" and "Lila Engel" encapsulate some of the same motorik, blurred, fuzzwhiteouts and descend into reverbed caverns and gentle atmospheres. "Gedenkminute": closeup breathing set in an ambience of funereal bells tolling across desolate, windy moors. "Neuschnee", gentler and more melodic, is reminiscent of the route Rother was to follow in his solo work and with Harmonia.

Contrary to popular belief, they did not run out of money halfway but because they didn't have enough material to fill a complete album after the available studio time was nearly used up, they rather decided on the 'deconstruction' of "Super" and "Neuschnee" as attention-grabbing-art-statement, feeling that they deserved better promotion than the one their label had given them on the single's release a few months earlier. They decided to "play around with it and put the results on side 2 of the album… Pop art thinking" (Dinger). First result: the first vinyl turntablism—their hit single, several times, at several speeds, non-concentric, swerving, modulated wobbliness, scratches and pops intact. Second result: "people thought we were making fun of them". [M Rother]

After the release of *NEU!2* Rother paid a visit to Cluster at their home in Forst, hoping to recruit them in an expanded live lineup of NEU! Jamming with Roedelius, Michael Rother discovered the great potential this collaboration had. He decided to put

NEU! on hold and moved to Forst to work with Roedelius and Moebius as Harmonia. Dinger, with his brother Thomas, and Hans Lampe formed La Düsseldorf.

In order to comply with their contract with Brain, Dinger and Rother were reunited to make *NEU!75*. Rother found an opportunity to make music he had developed at Forst but which he did not find suited for Harmonia. Considered by many to be their finest work, it has often been written that one side of *NEU!75* is Rother's and one is Dinger's: stylistically, both sides of the vinyl version are very different, it is true, but both are collaborations. "Without Klaus" says Rother " my ideas would have turned out quite different, without my contributions the tracks associated with Klaus would have become quite different too. It was the combination of our two strengths that made the magic."

On side 1, crystalline pianos echo across pulsing shuffling landscapes in "Isi", a beautiful, deceptively simple, melodic instrumental. The lullaby ambience of "Seeland" leads into the gorgeous "Leb Wohl" ["Farewell"], using water sounds and Dinger's whispered beachside nostalgia to create a tranquil, somnolent atmosphere. The two drum kits of Thomas Dinger and Hans Lampe launch side 2, lending a glittery edge to the tense, intense, raucous proto-punk of "Hero", "After Eight" and "E-musik", with Dinger's screaming vocals pushed, tense and intense, to the fore with Rother's fuzzed and processed guitar flying high. Less experimental that 1+2, this is the album that inspired many. Following its release, NEU! dissolved: Michael Rother released many great solo albums while Dinger continued his work with La Düsseldorf, both to significant commercial success.

NEU! reunited again in the studio in October 1985. Recordings were made in Düsseldorf and in Forst but the album *NEU! '86* was not completed. Due to their ongoing personal struggles and the lack of interest on the side of record companies, Dinger and Rother split the tapes and agreed to meet again at a later time to continue the project. In 1995, Klaus Dinger released (without Rother's consent) parts of their sessions with some additions (i.e. "86 Commercial Trash") under the name *NEU! 4*. Rother's attempts to find an agreement with Dinger for a legal and proper release of the project failed.

As it stands, *NEU!4* is an unfinished collection of television commercials excerpts, europop and national anthems, squelchy synths and reversed vocals drenched in reverb. Some unreleased material has, however, recently come to light [from Michael Rother's own mastertapes] which may finally complete the album also known as *NEU!86*. Grönland Records will release a vinyl box-set with the three "original" albums plus an album with Michael Rother's selection and edits of their recordings for *NEU!86*. The new version of the album as well as edits of a live rehearsal dating from 1972 will be released with the consent of Klaus Dinger's heir and last companion Miki Yui.

There probably is no other band like NEU!: their history is as complex and multi-faceted as their music. Rother says he had to undergo an "intellectual process of forgetting" in order to create a sound that was genuinely innovative. The politics and culture of the early 1970s made Rother realise that he needed to "forget the clichés, everything you had grown up with". They stripped rock music of all bloated, ostentatious ornamentation and reduced it to its purest essence: the almost tangible experience of perpetual forward motion through repetition and subtle variation.

Many of the bands of the early 1970s Krautrock scene recorded in their own studios—thus escaping the limits of fashion and record company pressure—to create a music still fresh and relevant today. It is this insistence on creating new forms which gave birth to NEU!'s timeless sound and is Krautrock's most significant legacy.

LM

Klaus Dinger. Courtesy Miki Yui.

POPOL VUH

Florian Fricke's Popol Vuh—taking their name from a Mayan creation myth—were the ultimate manifestation of Rolf Ulrich-Kaiser's vision of a new Kosmische Musik even as they exploded and eventually dispensed with all of its central tenets. Across the space of three decades they pioneered a form of devotional music that drew on middle-European classical traditions and the polyphony of early music as much as mind-erasing drones and Gnostic psychedelic modes. They began as a trio in 1970, with Fricke joined by Holger Trülzsch and Frank Fiedler. Their debut album *Affenstunde*, released by Liberty in the same year, is a one-off in their back catalogue, an attempt to translate modal Eurasian arrangements to Moog synthesizers and early electronics with elemental hand-drum patterns levitating the whole group off the face of the earth. For their second album they relocated to Kaiser's newly acquired cosmic folk label, Pilz, and came into their own with the release of *In Den Garten Pharaos* (1972) a milestone in the history of German psychedelic rock. Consisting of two side long pieces, the second piece, "Vuh", remains one of the highlights of their catalogue, a monolithic mass for church organ and triumphant crashing cymbals. But it's 1973's *Hosianna Mantra* that establishes the blueprint for the bulk of their career. With a title that deliberately conflates Hindu and Christian terminology, *Hosianna Mantra* was Fricke's attempt to mint a form of religious music that would transcend dogma while responding with reverence and awe to the miracle of consciousness and creation. Fricke also made the decision to abandon the easy mystic shorthand of endless electricity and F/X by moving towards a more ornate and delicately-nuanced acoustic style. The addition of Korean vocalist Djong Yun and ex-Gila guitarist Conny Veit sealed the changes. Yun's high, otherworldly vocals take the place of Fricke's cosmic organ settings while Veit's pure guitar tone works as a counterpoint to the stately piano arrangements. *Hosianna Mantra* remains one of the classic Krautrock recordings, perfectly balanced between virtuosity and simplicity, with Fricke and Veit reputedly spending six months working on the arrangements. In 1973 Veit reactivated Gila as a surrogate Popol Vuh that were capable of playing live

and Fricke joined him for the recording of their 1973 LP, *Bury My Heart At Wounded Knee*, where he met Daniel Fichelscher who would eventually replace Veit as his main collaborator. The group followed up the success of *Hosianna Mantra* with a thematically linked series of recordings that condensed and reformulated its various breakthroughs, 1974's *Seligpreisung* and 1975's *Einsjäger & Siebenjäger* and *Das Hohelied Salomos*. All three LPs can be seen as re-statements of aspects of *Hosianna Mantra*, with only *Das Hohelied Salomos* coming close to matching the liturgical beauty of its predecessor, thanks in no small part to Yun's inspired vocal performance. *Einsjäger & Siebenjäger* saw Popol Vuh settle down to the core duo of Fricke and Fichelscher, a partnership that would persist almost to the very end. 1976's *Letzte Tage—Letzte Nächte* saw them joined by Renate Knaup of Amon Düül II and reverse into the heavier environs of classic Krautrock before heading back to the future with Yoga later that same year, an album of Indian music featuring Fricke jamming on harmonium and organ with a group of classical Indian musicians. During the mid-1970s Fricke also became heavily involved with the film maker Werner Herzog, contributing soundtracks to films like *Aguirre, The Wrath Of God*, *Nosferatu* and *The Enigma Of Kaspar Hauser*, in which he also starred as a blind pianist. Although the music from the films was marketed as soundtrack albums, they stand on their own as some of the best Popol Vuh LPs, especially 1975's *Aguirre*, which opens with some of the most perfectly realized cosmic/religious music of their career, and 1978's *Nosferatu*. *Brüder Des Schattens, Söhne Des Lichts*, released the same year as *Nosferatu* and also featuring music commissioned for the soundtrack, inaugurates the last great phase of Popol Vuh, moving towards a more contemplative and ritualistic style while still functioning as a beautiful transport. Particular highlights from this incarnation include 1979's *Die Nacht Der Seele*, where Fricke was rejoined by both Knaup and Djong Yun, the eerie, occult ritual of 1981's *Sei Still, Wisse ICH BIN*, produced by Klaus Schulze, and the rapturous vocal levitations of 1985's perfectly-titled *Spirit Of Peace*. In the late 1980s Fricke began to introduce sampling keyboards and aspects of the new electronica into the Popol Vuh sound with increasingly diminishing returns. By the time of 1995's *City Raga* and 1997's *Shepherd's Symphony*, Fricke's latest collaborator, Guido Hieronymus, had effectively reduced the group to an unfortunate techno caricature. Fricke passed away peacefully, in his sleep, on 29th December 2001 a few days after suffering a stroke. He is remembered—by fans as diverse as Kate Bush and Julian Cope—as a visionary musician who created some of the most awe-inspiring and creatively ambitious music to come out of the German rock revolution.

DK

From left to right: Conny Veit, Robert Eliscu, Florian Fricke. Courtesy Eurock Archives.

Guitarist, actor, teenage pin-up, countercultural visionary… Achim Reichel's trip is one of the longest and strangest in Krautrock history. Reichel was an original member of Germany's best loved beat group The Rattles, who supported The Beatles in 1966. But Reichel was already demonstrating the restless spirit that would define the rest of his career and after the Beatles shows he split to form his own rock group, Wonderland, with Rattles member Frank Dorstal. As Wonderland Band they recorded a single 1971 LP for Polydor that combined the usurping humor of Frank Zappa and The Mothers Of Invention with schizophrenic forays into genre. However it's the run of albums that Reichel recorded under the name Achim Reichel & Machines that are best loved by fans of mutant sounds. The first album, 1971's *Die Grune Reise*, issued by Polydor, is a good amalgam of echo-guitar based space rock and straightahead boogie blasters but it was the wildly ambitious follow-up, 1972's double LP *Echo*, that really nailed him to the map. *Echo* stands alongside Walter Wegmüller's *Tarot*, Ash Ra Tempel's

Schwingungen, Sergius Golowin's *Krishna Von Goloka* and the early works of Klaus Schulze as a classic of questing psychedelic gnosis. Intended as an eschatological concept album that would refract visions of the past and future through the technology of now, *Echo* boasted an orchestral line-up that included Klaus Schulze and legendary producer Conny Plank on vocals. As the title suggests, the whole album is saturated in F/X, with vocals surging into warped high-masses while guitars thread odd, ethnic melodies through a soup of reverb and delay. 1972's *AR3* was a slight reprise of the endlessly reflective sound of *Echo* while *AR 4* and *5* (1973 and 1974 respectively) effected a comparative reconciliation with standard rock form. From the late 1970s onwards Reichel turned his talents more towards the mainstream and a burgeoning career as an actor but there are still some corners of the world that continue to recognise him as the crackpot behind one the wiggiest trips of the German rock revolution.

DK

Achim Reichel with The Rattles, 1965. Photo: Siggi Loch.

ACHIM REICHEL

GAVIN RUSSOM
ON ACHIM REICHEL

I've been spending a lot of time with Achim Reichel's music lately. In mid–2007 a friend suggested that Reichel's AR & Machines project might be an interesting reference point for a transition I was making in the way I write music. I had begun to work with the guitar again for the first time in almost 15 years, having spent most of my career exploring the secrets of designing, building and playing analog synthesizers. Although I didn't know it at the time, I had already heard Reichel's most well-known work "Aloha He Ja". I was taking a detour through Berlin's Tiergarten during a pre-game rally for the European Cup finals and it was playing on the large outdoor PA. I was struck by the melody and mood of the song. It sounded both haunting and uplifting. The reedy keyboard emerging from the repetitive and steady bassline created a sense of triumph through change that I have come to associate with a certain kind of European pop. It's something I draw on frequently in my own work, so I scribbled a note to myself that I still have, "Find track that says 'Ich sag Zanzibar'". At first listen I related to both the expansive sound of Reichel's guitar work with AR & Machines and the clean and driving feel of the pop song, but wouldn't have imagined that both came from the same source. Reconciling these seemingly incompatible sensibilities is one of the challenges I consistently face in my own work, and Reichel's ability to do so has become a welcome model.

When I began to look at Reichel's career in depth, I felt an instant sense of recognition. I like the free-wheeling, "cut loose" sound of his early beat group The Rattles. The music is aggressive and dreamy at the same time and has an energy that I hear emerging later in LA punk groups like The Germs, who were one of the first influences on my musical development. The video for "Love's a Murder" by his later group Wonderland is so eerily like some of my early performances with artist and musician Delia Gonzalez, such as *The Other Side* or *Mujer o Monstro*, that I find it hard to believe we didn't take directly from it at the time.

Of course, the recordings that Reichel made with AR & Machines were exactly the kind of inspiration I needed to translate the language of synth sequences and arpeggios into more hand-played guitar work. Throughout the 1970s, Reichel uses a similar kind of trance-inducing repetition to his fellow space travelers. The difference is that his songs have a theatricality about them that also brings them down to earth.

When I began working with group improvisation in my late teens I was searching for exactly the kind of compositional idiom that Reichel turns into an art form on the "Machines" recordings. Pink Floyd's *Ummagumma* was my major touchstone at the time. The issue that I ran into, that shifted me more towards electronics was that in the end every song yielded by group improv seemed to sound just about the same. There was always just one energy curve. Reichel's music transcends this limitation. Each of his compositions tells a unique story, but still retains the quality of organic development and spontaneous abstraction that comes with the territory. Sometimes the story is obvious, like in "Aqua—Every Raindrop Longs For The Sea". There, a constantly changing field recording of water follows the bubbling guitar lines and guides us from a mountain rainstorm through lakes and rivers and lastly into the waves, as the sounds merge into one another. In a track like "Eisenpferde", though, there are no direct references at all, but the churning guitar and blaring sax create, for me as I listen, the strong sense of movement on some kind of great and powerful machine.

I have no idea what happened during the transition between the 1970s and the 1980s. I was quite young at the time but it seems that huge changes in musical sensibility happened almost overnight. Reichel also changed dramatically. On the surface a slick production like "Der Spieler", his 1982 hit, and a sprawling journey like the epic "Einladung (Invitation)" from A.R. & Machines IV, have almost nothing in common. In fact they seem to be at such opposite ends of a certain aesthetic spectrum that it's hard to believe the same person wrote them. As I listen more deeply, though, it is again Reichel's ability to achieve a narrative quality through his relationship to melody and repetition that links the works produced in these two periods.

Although Reichel's guitar work itself has been a great inspiration to me, it is this sense of the theatrical and the ability to occupy many genres while retaining a signature sound that is what I keep coming back to. Viewed from this perspective his career is more like a deepening of certain themes (a particular fascination with the sea, for example). He's been able to stay flexible and consistently develop these themes as times have changed, his stories becoming more defined in the process. This approach maintains the integrity of both an inner world of dreams, inspirations and obsessions, and the outer world of progress, and invention. In my own music, continually working with this dichotomy is one of the most challenging and rewarding parts of the composing experience. Reichel has been able to work with it over a career of over 40 years. At this point in my listening, 1998's "Aloha He Ja" no longer sounds like a departure from the earlier cosmic works, rather it is like their essence; a refined crystal moment carefully hewn out of one man's dream of adventure.

CONRAD SCHNITZLER

Unlike many of Krautrock's most noted practitioners, Conrad Schnitzler, once dubbed "the untameable experimentalist", did not spend the 1960s playing in Beatles-type beat groups or doing cover versions for pennies. Although he was a student of Stockhausen, and keenly aware of the music of John Cage and Pierre Schaeffer, he was not a "musician" as such, more of a finder, an arranger and a maker of sounds. Born in 1937, his training was in art. He studied sculpture under Joseph Beuys in his home town of Düsseldorf in the 1960s and thereafter brought a conceptual artist's sensibility to bear on the experimental German scene, which, despite his own lack of any formal training on any instrument, proved highly educative to his more proficient peers.

Schnitzler had a distaste for the hippy-ish domination of drums and flute in late 1960s German music and for anything that resembled anything so sickly cloying as a tune. "A melody is like a worm in your head", he would later say. His preference was for sounds that went "in and out" and his lack of any cosy adherence to any particular model, mode of expression or idiom is a reflection of this philosophy—as well as his uncommonly vast discography. Over the years, the amount of sound he has generated, in the form of field recordings, untrammelled electronics, treated instruments, pre-recorded cassettes, defies cataloguing. In one year alone in the 1980s, he produced 14 albums' worth of material. Doubtless much more has never seen the light of day, including the signed copy of unreleased material he once sent to a fan by correspondence, with his compliments.

Schnitzler was one of the key founders of the Zodiak Free Arts Lab in Berlin. He recalled how when they first played, for several days, no one came because no one knew it existed. Only then did it occur to them to leaflet local concerts, whereupon the venue became a vortex not just for disaffected young rockers but also free jazz luminaries such as Peter Brötzmann and Alexander Von Schlippenbach, all working together in a haze of dope.

Having initially formed a group by the name of Geräusche (Noises), whose manifesto was that "if lots of people make noise it

Conrad Schnitzler at the Zodiak. Courtesy Conrad Schnitzler. Photo: Werner Strey.

becomes an orchestra", and being one of the trio on Tangerine Dream's debut album *Electronic Meditation*, in which he taught Edgar Froese some startling lessons about thinking outside the musical box, Schnitzler went on to form Kluster, whose 1971 albums *Klopfzeichen* and *Zwei Osterei* (the latter conceived thanks to the interest of a local churchman, hence its religious theme) were brutalist works in which conventional instruments were (mis) treated to gruelling yet strangely beautiful work, anticipating the works of Throbbing Gristle, Einstürzende Neubauten and, later, the pure electronic noisenik Merzbow. On leaving Kluster, fellow members Dieter Moebius and Hans Roedelius dropped the harsh "K" of "Kluster" for a softer "C" and dramatically adjusted their music accordingly.

Schnitzler, by contrast, went his own way. His solo output is too vast to do justice to in a few short paragraphs but

Courtesy Conrad Schnitzler. Photo: Jürgen Müller-Schneck.

standouts include 1973's *Rot*, part of a series of colour-based releases. Recorded in late 1972 in an old cellar once used by Tangerine Dream for rehearsals, it was released in a limited edition of 500 in 1973. Its two tracks are harsh, decidedly anti-kosmische. "Meditation" is like the systematic dismantling or falling apart of an electronic sound machine, with springs flying, gaskets bursting and screws pinging out of their holes. "Krautrock", meanwhile, is like a German soundlab in which the balaclava'd outsider Schnitzler has broken in through the window and, like a member of the Noise Liberation Front, set free scrapes, squeals and drones from any formal musical context for which they were being prepared. Again, it anticipates later developments in rock, particularly Cabaret Voltaire's "Johnny Yesno" to which it bears uncanny similarities.

1978's *Ballet Statique* is, by contrast, a rhythm based excursion into an electropop of sorts, all blasts and bleeps and very big with later collage/beatmakers like Mixmaster Morris. 1989's *Constellations*, meanwhile, is Schnitzler working on a symphonic scale, a mountainous epic piled high with samples, tapes and synths, sped up, filtered and remixed.

Schnitzler is one of the undersung and tireless heroes of Krautrock, who has imported the conceptual values of contemporary art into music, when it might have been a good deal more expedient (and lucrative) for him to have stuck to his sculpting. Documentary footage of him collecting his field recordings and found sounds from around Berlin in the 1970s shows him wandering the streets with a boom mic above his head, as if as much a torchbearer for the present day avant-garde artist as a musician at work. In some ways, Schnitzler himself is the work of art.
DS

A veteran of the late 1960s wave of Berlin experimentation and, more recently, a collaborator with ambient/electronic artist Pete Namlook, Klaus Schulze has been active and prolific for four uninterrupted decades. While his music has been enhanced and upgraded, matured and developed over the years, the work which still represents the greatest, unearthly challenge to the modern listener is his earliest.

Klaus Schulze was born in Berlin, the city most pivotal to his music, in 1947. During the 1960s, he served the usual apprenticeship of his generation, playing various instruments, and primarily drums, in a variety of local groups, getting down pat the orthodox rock and pop styles from which he would so dramatically depart in his early 20s. From about 1968 onwards, and after having studied with Swiss avant-garde composer Thomas Kessler, Schulze began making tapes of his own experimental music. Unsurprisingly, he jumped at the chance of playing at the Zodiak Free Arts Lab, attracted by the venue in that its location allowed you to play as loudly as possible without the risk of public complaint. Almost immediately, he fell in with Edgar Froese and Conrad Schnitzler, with whom he made up the first line-up of Tangerine Dream. But disagreements with Froese in particular led him to join Ash Ra Tempel, with whom he went on to record on and off in the early 1970s.

However, it was with 1972's first solo album *Irrlicht* that he made his 'Big Bang' record, the impact of which has yet to be properly absorbed today. Deriving from ideas he had discussed but failed to agree upon with Froese, *Irrlicht* predated Tangerine Dream's broadly similar *Zeit* by a month or so. But *Irrlicht* was a more eventful attempt than *Zeit*, with its fadeouts, eruptions, supernovae and black holes; drawing for its sound sources, via distorting filters, on organ and a full orchestra, it had more in common with Stockhausen's 1960 composition *Kontakte*, representing one of the closest meeting points between rock and musique concrète.

1973's *Cyborg* followed, another kosmische excursion in which rock is left behind like the planet earth itself. It has echoes of both Can and Faust, in its grainy fuzztones and dub-like reverb. Death rattles, particle showers and analogue synth tones spiral through a space recently vacated for good by the American Apollo project, as if surveying the aftermath and debris.

Come 1974 and the fine *Blackdance*, Schulze's hardware is becoming recognisably electronic. There are vocals, echoes of Pink Floyd's "Set The Controls For The Heart Of The Sun" and as with Tangerine Dream the same year,

Klaus Schulze in Paris, 1978. Photo: Christian Piednoir.

you sense the beginnings of a commercial gravitational pull. *Picture Music*, with its pretty arabesques, pre-sequencer percussive patter and serene, LP side-long odysseys, sees Schulze in the full swing of his "Berlin School" phase, in which his music has become codified, with warm guitar, synth and mellotron tones counter-pointed by cold, impersonal rhythms. This was perfected on 1976's *Moondawn*, considered by many to be Schulze's masterpiece and certainly an apotheosis of sorts in its accomplished and well-travelled trans-lunar bliss. Schulze was not quite so "out there" any more but in there with the likes of Steve Winwood and Stomu Yamashta's 1976 album *Go*.

In the 1980s, Schulze's commercial and artistic fate was sealed with the onset of the sequencer and digital sequencer—once again in parallel with Tangerine Dream. The albums he made during this period hardly push back the envelope but are pleasing enough if you forgive their accessibility

and their hovering towards the new age category in the record racks. Schulze did, however, in the 1990s, experiment with sampling, which disconcerted some of his fans. He dropped this, in favour of what had become a more tried and trusted formula. He has certainly been extraordinary prolific, recording well over 40 albums under his own name as well as recordings under the name of Richard Wahnfried and collaborations with Pete Namlook on the long-running, Pink Floyd-parodying Dark Side Of The Moog series. Taken as a whole, his body of work represents electronic abundance. However, the abiding appeal and strangeness of his early work comes from its primitivism, which doesn't sound predated or naïve but freer, more desolate and inquisitive, less hidebound by the grids and conventions of technological development. *Irrlicht* in particular burns brighter than ever almost three decades on.

DS

Klaus Schulze at the Hippodrome, Paris, 1978. Photo: Christian Piednoir.

SPACEBOX/ ULI TREPTE

Like Can drummer Jaki Liebezeit, bassist Uli Trepte came out of the German free jazz scene, playing in a trio with Guru Guru drummer Mani Neumeier and pianist Irene Schweizer from 1966–67. After switching from acoustic to electric bass he formed the ultimate Krautrock power trio, Guru Guru, whose music channelled wild improvisatory energy into a monosyllabic form of two-chord psychedelic redux, with caveman rhythms giving way to endless space jams. After quitting the group in 1972, Trepte formed his own improvisational rock group, Kickbit Information, and moonlighted with both NEU! and Faust. It was while touring with the latter in the UK that Trepte introduced his 'Spacebox', a shortwave radio with electronic effects that sounded like a wonky umbilical to Venus. Trepte assembled his next group around the sound of his invention, naming it Spacebox and recruiting Julius Golombeck on guitar, Edgar Hofmann on saxophone, violin and flute, Winfried Beck on drums and congas and Lotus Schmidt on drums and gongs. Spacebox's 1981 self-titled debut, issued privately by Trepte himself, is a ferocious amalgam of amphetamine punk, overdriven amplifier worship and loose improvisatory structures. The manic energy levels were hard to maintain and by the time of its follow-up, 1984's *Kick Up*, the group had settled into a slightly more straightforward jam-based style, with touches of the ethno stylings of fellow travelers Embryo. In 1985 Trepte hooked-up with Steven Stapleton of the UK Industrial group Nurse With Wound to record an ill-fated Spacebox album, all but blighted by Trepte's increasingly eccentric behavior in the studio. In the end it was issued as *Hot On Spot/Inbetween*, a split LP on United Dairies that paired studio recordings of a Spacebox line-up that featured Christian Burchard and Roman Bunka of Embryo with a live rendition of Guru Guru's "Bo Diddley". In the wake of the dissolution of Spacebox, Trepte put together a song-based project under the name *Takes On Words* and until the end of his life he was still jamming with friends as part of Move Groove. He died on 21st May 2009 after a long struggle with cancer.

DK

Uli Trepte (front) with Winfried Beck (left). Courtesy of Eurock Archives. Photo: Roland Fischer.

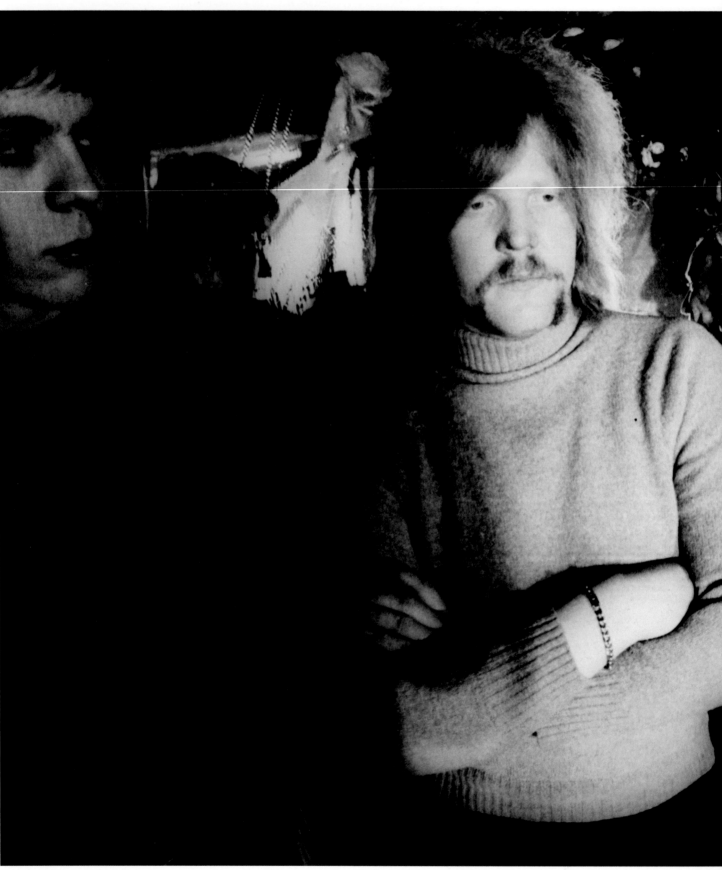

Early Tangerine Dream. From left to right: Klaus Schulze, Edgar Froese, Conrad Schnitzler. Courtesy Wolfgang Seidel. Photo: Wilfried Bauer.

For many, Tangerine Dream are synonymous, in an amused sort of way not unlike Yes, with electronic prog/1970s music. Even though they came to synthesizers later than others, they are vaguely regarded as arch-perpetrators of electronic pseudo-symphonies stretching across many sides of gatefold sleeved albums, traversing vast, cosmic tracts of pretentiousness.

The truth is rather more complex. Tangerine Dream's discography is vast but it is their early, "Pink" years which make them of primary interest. They have resisted and resented the tag "new age" and with just cause, as the term is inherently empty, but there is no doubt that their later music has enjoyed a commercial success in direct proportion to its reassuringly balmy, sequencer driven patterns. All of that said, it would be foolish not to explore Tangerine Dream either on the basis of their later work or their shorthand reputation. The awning of albums like *Zeit*, misunderstood and even derided at the time of its release, still hangs high and significant today.

Tangerine Dream's line-up has shifted greatly over the years but the common factor has always been Edgar Froese. Born in East Prussia at the end of the Second World War, Froese studied art in Berlin and sculpture in the mid-1960s but also formed a beat group called The Ones, who eked out a precarious living playing familiar standards like "In The Midnight Hour" over and over, travelling Europe and subsisting on the cheapest food available. It was during one such tour, in Spain, that Froese met the Surrealist painter Salvador Dalí at his villa in Cadaqués. Marvelling at the extravagantly unorthodox manner in which the artist conducted himself, Froese experienced an epiphany—it was as if his soundworld had turned to colour and the straight, grey lines of orthodox, Anglo-American orientated beat music had been breached forever. He returned to Berlin, took up the moniker Tangerine Dream, in which colour and imagination were suitably married, and dropped in at the recently founded Zodiak Arts Lab, during which he exercised his new free-form, spatial awareness participating in six hour improvised gigs.

The first Tangerine Dream album was called *Electronic Meditation*, recorded in a rented factory space with fellow Zodiak denizens Conrad Schnitzler and drummer Klaus Schulze. (There are also two other previously uncredited musicians: organist Jimmy Jackson and flautist Thomas Keyserling.) Recorded on two-track, the "Electronic" tag is a misnomer, as in fact most of the instruments are conventional ones unconventionally treated—it was "electronic" in spirit only. The main trio integrated perfectly. Schulze's tumultuous percussion, uncomplemented by bass, rained down freely from on high, while Froese on guitar, piano and tapes, unbound by pop strictures, was flanked by Schnitzler, unbound by any sort of practice in, or ability to play "proper" music at all. Rather, Schnitzler extracted noises from the cello and played the typewriter, or contributed 'found sounds' derived from broken glass or dried peas, like random but crucial elements in a visual collage. It was the perfect continuum. Too perfect, however—three such strong willed characters could not be tethered together for long and for the next album, a new set of musicians including Peter Baumann and Christopher Franke entered the ranks. It was here that Froese's vision of "kosmische musik" began to be realised in earnest, as reflected in the album's title. Franke, meanwhile, brought with him a knowledge of contemporary classical music such as Ligeti which further enhanced Tangerine Dream's dimensions.

Zeit (1972) is perhaps the most extreme undertaking, the true voyage to the Dark Side Of The Moon, one which puts Pink Floyd's own declared efforts in this vein in their proper perspective as cosy, shagpile amateur astronomers by comparison. It's based on the notion that all is actually motionless and that the concept of time only exists in our minds. Tangerine Dream go some way in realising this notion of absolute, universal stasis, across beatless tracks, luxuriating in the inscrutable void, in which drones fold back on themselves and the stem sawing of the Cologne Cello Quartet casts giant interplanetary shadows. To call this album prog is a nonsense, as, more than any other rock album of the time, it explicitly and profoundly negates the idea of "progress" altogether.

Atem, the 1973 follow up, was more eventful by comparison. Still located in remote outer space, it nonetheless featured busy percussion, like the furious phutting of a spacecraft outboard motor, and the pervasive, sepia tint of the mellotron, particularly on "Fauni-Gena", with its solemnly utopian, hanging gardens of keyboard. John Peel voted *Atem* his album of the year for 1973—a well meant but fateful decision, perhaps, as this raised the interest of inadvertent Krautrock nemesis Richard Branson. He signed the group to his Virgin label and, while 1974's *Phaedra* is a fine album, echoes of which can be heard in, for example, the work of contemporary Japanese artist Kawabata Makoto, you can already hear Froese & co scampering towards commercial coherence. Once the sequencer was introduced the game was up. Despite enormous success, much of Tangerine's Dream's post-"Pink" work comes across as Vangelis-like cinematic soundtracking, evoking images of horses galloping across clifftop fields shot from a helicopter and so forth.

Despite falling out of fashion in the 1980s, this is when Tangerine Dream were at their busiest in many ways, particularly producing soundtracks, taking advantage of the digital technology which they had prefigured, but no longer confounding or extending the vocabulary of such music. They soundtracked the likes of *The Sorcerer*, *The Keep* and *Risky Business*, and it's thanks to this work alone that Tangerine Dream found an altogether new audience. Come the 1990s and the advent of trance, Tangerine Dream received their dues and compliments from bands such as Future Sound Of London. Edgar's son Jerome Froese, who had featured on the cover of *Atem*, would eventually become a member of the group himself. Things finally came full circle.

DS

Tangerine Dream   Virgin Records

Virgin-era Tangerine Dream. Courtesy Eurock Archives.

WALTER WEGMÜLLER

Swiss gypsy and folk magician Walter Wegmüller is best loved by fans of kosmische music for the single album issued under his name, 1972's sprawling double LP *Tarot*. The seed of the *Tarot* album came from scenester, critic and visionary rock theorist Rolf-Ulrich Kaiser as he fever-dreamed a series of supergroup jams led by oracular frontmen. With acid evangelist Timothy Leary holed up in the white hills and on the run from the CIA, Ulrich set him up as the first featured vocalist, backed by Ash Ra Tempel for the recording of the *7Up* album. The second phase of the cosmic supersessions involved poet, green politician and mystic Sergius Golowin, while the third featured Wegmüller, who, at Leary's urging, developed a suite of songs and instrumentals based around musical reifications of the powers and personalities of the Tarot. Wegmüller had been working for several years on his own hand-painted interpretation, a deck that had a particular folkloric bent. The Tarot sessions brought together one of the heaviest big-band line-ups in the history of Krautrock, with Wegmüller joined by Jerry Berkers and Jürgen Dollase of Wallenstein, Hartmut Enke, Manuel Göttsching, Rosi Muller and Harald Grosskopf of Ash Ra Tempel, Walter Westrupp of Witthüser & Westrupp, producer Dieter Dierks and keyboardist/vocalist Klaus Schulze. Across the space of the two LPs there is a track dedicated to each of the major arcana, running from Wegmüller's goof-off intro for "The Fool" through the martial acid guitar of "The Emperor" to Klaus Schulze's faltering schoolboy vocal on "The Hermit". *Tarot* is a massively ambitious work that provides the blueprint for subsequent attempts to mint a religio-magickal form of devotional music. There's a primitive quality to much of the interaction—dud notes and wayward solos—that gives it an inspirational punk feel, while the advanced studio process and insane panning and phasing make it the ultimate in hallucinatory headphone trips. Easily one of the most powerful recordings to come out of the whole Rolf-Ulrich Kaiser/Cosmic Couriers saga, *Tarot* has been reissued several times, once with a complete reproduction of Wegmüller's Tarot pack. In the wake of the *Tarot* recordings, Wegmüller went on to establish himself as a successful visual artist.

DK

Walter Wegmüller. Courtesy Heidi Ramseier.

Witthüser and Westrupp's 1971 album, *Trips und Träume*, is one of the most perfectly odd recordings ever to come out of extended experiments with psychedelics. In its combination of Bavarian folk simplicity and endless euphoric drones it is exemplary of that most fugitive of genres, acid-folk. Bernd Witthüser and Walter Westrupp both came out of the German folk club scene in the mid-1960s. They met at the Podium folk club in Essen, a venue that Witthüser managed and where Westrupp was a DJ. Their first album together, 1970's *Lieder Von Vampiren, Nonnen Und Toten*, was actually billed as a Witthüser solo album and despite the fact that it was issued by Ohr it's actually a fairly ordinary traditional folk record. But sometime in late 1970 or early 1971 the duo seemed to have gone through some kind of psychedelic initiation with the result that their music became suddenly illuminated. With the boosting of underground evangelist Rolf-Ulrich Kaiser,

they cut a trio of albums that trailblazed a singular synthesis of traditional European folk music and dosed acid rock. *Trips Und Träume* remains their masterpiece, the perfect amalgam of dopey paeans to the joys of hash and extended hymns to oblivion that are as beautifully deep as anything by Ash Ra Tempel. Their second album, 1972's *Der Jesuspilz*, was a concept album based around then-popular notions of Christianity as a magic mushroom cult while their third and final studio effort, 1972's *Bauer Path*, featured collaborations from Wallenstein and saw the duo bolster their cosmic folk sound with more rock-based arrangements. The same year, Westrupp participated in Walter Wegmüller's classic German psych summit, *Tarot*, before the duo parted company for good, with nothing but a retrospective live album as a memorial to one of the most original folk duos this side of the Incredible String Band.

DK

Bernd Witthüser (left) with Walter Westrupp (far right) in their farm in Dill, Germany. Courtesy Walter WEstrupp.

WITTHÜSER & WESTRUPP

To hear early 'soul', you had to search among the high numbers at the far end of the radio dial, among obscure Black stations. For 'Xhol', the numbers had to go astronomically high and further out. You also had to listen on WDR, rather than something coming out of a shack in Louisville or Detroit.

There was a connection, though. In 1967, two German saxophonists Tim Belbe and Hansi Fischer formed a Motown covers band called Soul Caravan. Fischer was from Wiesbaden, Belbe born a year later in 1944 at Bad Schwalbach, half an hour to the north west. Like others who grew up in the US-occupied zone, an instinct for American music was genetically imprinted and an exposure to it virtually guaranteed. Some measure of authenticity was delivered by two American singers, James Rhodes and Ronny Swinton, who joined the first version of Soul Caravan, but neither their competent vocals nor an almost cartoonishly 'soulful' bass line disguised a sense, confirmed on release of *Get In High*, that the band had an other, more experimental agenda. Released on CBS at a time when the label's European subsidiaries had considerable creative autonomy and were thus able to express the creative interests and avant-garde sensibilities of some executives, *Get In High* is still an extraordinary achievement. Though its programme is song-based and a hybrid of r'n'b and soul, the music is informed by strong psychedelic elements and hints of a more free-form approach that were either influenced by or evolved parallel to developments in German free jazz at the period. Heard repeatedly, it is an album that seems to dissolve rather than coalesce.

This tendency within the group was confirmed by a number of personnel changes over the following year but the personnel eventually settled round Ocki Brevert's unsettling organ sound—a hybrid of the Doors' Ray Manzarek and American Minimalism—bassist Klaus Briest from Wiesbaden and drummer Skip Vanwych, along with founders Belbe and Fischer, and with Rhodes as the soul survivor. Swinton left, along with short-term member, guitarist Werner Funk. Live performances became more extended and improvisatory, and the emerging style derived something from Pink Floyd and Soft Machine, though with fewer elements of whimsy, while also unexpectedly incorporating aspects of the Beach Boys' eclectic sound-palette, the Doors' long-form expeditions, Frank Zappa's flip-flop between freshman humour and symphonic rock, and the Grateful Dead's spooling, overlapping jams; in later years, as Xhol, the group's communitarian lifestyle and aesthetic and word-of-mouth reputation cemented an association with the Dead. An unexpected element of pastoral was introduced by Fischer's very distinctive flute and soprano playing, the latter often heavily processed to sound like anything from a shawm to a thick-stringed electric guitar.

After a year of concentrated activity, the group released a fine single on Hansa that suggested a permanent change of direction. So did the new group name, Xhol Caravan, subsequently shorted to Xhol. "Planet Earth" (b.w. "So Down") introduced a trippier sound, brooding but never monochrome, built up on long, rhythmic loops from the drums rather than a driving, motorik rhythm. The album that followed on the same label has some claim as the first Krautrock release. Whatever its claims on priority, *Electrip* is a key record of the period.

It begins, jarringly, with the sound of a flushing toilet, a neatly ambiguous gesture: is everything that follows to be regarded as disposable, just more cultural effluent from the backwash of post-war capitalism? Or does it represent a cleansing whirl that washes away much of what has gone before? Both interpretations work for "Electric Fun Fair", which presents a world controlled by what the Situationists of the time were calling "the spectacle" but also implying that life can be reduced to the hallucinatory simplicities heard later on "All Green", one of Xhol Caravan's very finest performances. "Pop Games" suggests a similar trajectory, a hyper vocal initially drawing attention away from the radical straightforwardness of the musical line. The long "Raise Up High" is more representative of the band's live, jamming approach, but what it gains in sheer mass and durational intensity, it loses in terms of structure, an undervalued element of Xhol Caravan's achievement.

The last quality wasn't necessarily in evidence on 1970's *Hau-ruck*, a live album consisting of two long and apparently shapeless jams. Integral to these, though, are contrasting elements that reflect at once a larky, unsolemn approach to the Doors' sexual libertarianism (or libertinism) and a sound practical understanding of the still-misrepresented relationship between Miles Davis' live electronic performances and the studio artefacts derived from them. Xhol's work—the "Caravan" was dropped just before *Hau-ruk*—emphasises neither 'product' nor 'process', but a kind of utopian mid-space that takes some elements from both and treats them with wry disregard. Belbe's saxophone, which in the past often played Dewey Redman to Fischer's more strident Ornette Coleman, is more evident here and more demonstrative.

The utopian strain is perhaps most effectively blended with the satirical on *Motherfuckers GMBH & CO KG*, also recorded in 1970, but not released for two years. The 'corporate' style is obviously self-debunking, but the music attains an extraordinary fragile balance between an affirmative psych-folk and the machine-made motor sound of some branches of Minimalism. Brevert's electric piano work on previous outings had merely underlined a comparison with Manzarek. Increasingly, though, his playing seemed to come from the same place as some of Steve Reich's early scores or La Monte Young's drone-based trance music, two approaches to what became known as Minimalist music that attempted to transcend the repetitious alienations of western society by re-appropriating repetition as an element of organic life, ritual and spiritual discipline respectively.

Motherfuckers… and the subsequent *Motherfuckers Live* (released only in 2001) bring the Xhol story to an effective close. A group not so much ahead of its time as so intuitively responsive to its time that its output seemed alien. A group whose very closeness of temperament—rather than the usual ego-differences—guaranteed its short-lived nature. Xhol's importance as one of the Ur-groups of Krautrock is undeniable, and yet the specific vectors of influence are highly complex. The hot buttered xhol of the earlier work—'early' only in the most relative terms, since they weren't around for long—is still notionally present in the dark psychedelia and gestural free jazz of the 'later' records. Somewhere in the airwaves there is a bandwidth occupied by Soft Machine's *Four*, the Doors' *Soft Parade*, Peter Brötzmann's *Machine Gun* and the Dead's *American Beauty*, all co-existing quietly or not so quietly. Like the Dead, and those others at their best, Xhol seemed to occupy a place in music that was beyond genre and with a philosophy of sound impenetrable to most of the industry's categorisers, whether label people or critics. Like the most singular of artists, Xhol was self-defining, a de-gospelized version of the American original, re-invested with European nature philosophy. **BM**

Xhol Caravan Motherfuckers Live + Hot Buttered Xhol, 2001.

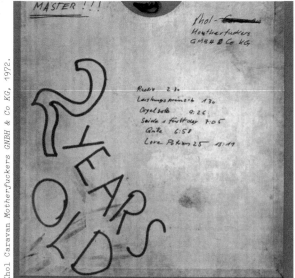

Xhol Caravan Motherfuckers GNBH & Co KG, 1972.

Xhol Caravan, *Electrip*, 1969.

Xhol Caravan live. Courtesy of Garden of Delights.

RECORD LABELS

BACILLUS

The Bacillus label was founded in 1971 by producer Peter Hauke, with Dieter Dierks as the engineer behind most of the label's releases. The label's roster contained, among others, Nine Days Wonder and Nektar, a German-based psychedelic group comprised entirely of English members. Although the label was briefly distributed by Polydor, Hauke managed to secure a distribution deal with Bellaphon (which was founded in 1961 by Branco Zivanovic and had made its reputation in the reliable and busy fields of beat and folk music). Amongst the most hugely popular Bacillus/Bellaphon releases, were the 1973 Nektar concept album *Remember The Future* as well as several records by the very successful band Omega, a Hungarian prog rock group whose albums for Bacillus were often English re-recordings of their Hungarian songs. Message, a German-British progressive rock band, whose 1972 album *The Dawn Anew is Coming* featured Nektar's Taff Freeman, also recorded for the label. Between 1971–1979, Dierks and Hauke worked together on the production, recording and release of 60 albums.

1 Bacillus/Bellaphon 19064, 1971.
2 Bacillus/Bellaphon BLPS 19118, 1972.
3 Bacillus/Bellaphon BLPS 19159 Q, 1973.
4 Bacillus/Bellaphon BLPS 19161 Q, 1973.
5 Bacillus/Bellaphon BLPS 19164, 1973.
6 Bacillus/Bellaphon BDA 7501, 1973.

1

6

3

5

4

2

BRAIN

Due to a dissatisfaction with the methods of Ohr records founder Rolf-Ulrich Kaiser, Bruno Wendel and Günter Körber, decided to leave Ohr and set up Brain, as a subdivision of the major Hamburg label Metronome. Metronome, an independent label that had briefly distributed Ohr and that had also released Amon Duul's *Collapsing* and *Psychedelic Underground* in 1969 was keen to respond to the increasing demand for progressive/psychedelic music in Germany. Brain inaugurated with the 1972 release of the Scorpions' album *Lonesome Crow*. Having already taken Guru Guru with them, the label was further bolstered by the signing of Klaus Schulze and also Cluster, whose adoption of the soft "C" signified a more listener-friendly, though still radical approach to music-making. The Brain logo was a wonderful 1970s conceit, the outline of a human face squiggling up into the word "Brain" arranged in such a way graphically as to look like an open cerebellum. The period between its inauguration in 1972 and 1976 was Brain's golden era; under its legendary 1000 series the label released 58 original German records including such landmarks as the three NEU! albums, Cluster's *Zuckerzeit* and Harmonia's *Deluxe*, as well as albums by Klaus Schulze, Grobschnitt, Eroc, and Edgar Froese.. Their output became increasingly diverse, licensing a number of British albums by Caravan, If, Spirogyra, Alexis Korner, Gryphon and Steamhammer for the West German market. All Brain albums were distinguished by their green labels but the colour switched to orange when Günter Körber left in 1975 to found Sky Records.

1

1 Brain/Metronome 1021, 1972.
2 Brain/Metronome 1023, 1973.
3 Brain/Metronome 1025, 1973.
4 Brain/Metronome 1007, 1972.
5 Brain/Metronome 1004, 1972.
6 Brain/Metronome 1062, 1974.
7 Brain/Metronome 1028, 1973.

2

3

4

5

6

7

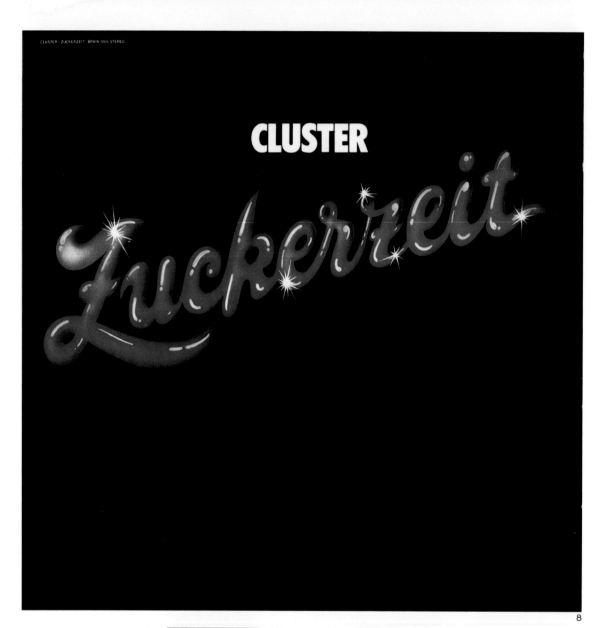

8

9

8 Brain/Metronome 1065, 1974.
9 Brain/Metronome 1006, 1972.
10 Brain/Metronome 60.117, 1978.
11 Brain/Metronome 1068, 1975. .
12 Brain/Metronome 1069, 1975.
13 Brain/Metronome 1073, 1975.

10

11

12

13

14

KOSMISCHE MUSIK

Rolf-Ulrich Kaiser created Kosmische Kuriere (which was almost instantly renamed Kosmische Musik) as an offshoot/successor of Ohr. Unlike the wild eclecticism of the latter, Kosmische Musik's output was more coherent, releasing some of the more far-out albums in the whole Krautrock scene. Inspired by their encounters with Timothy Leary, Albert Hoffman, HR Geiger, Walter Wegmüller and Sergius Golowin, and driven by their vision of a music tuned to the vibrations of the universe, Kaiser and his wife Gille Lettmann conceived of a label merging electronics, acid folk, cosmic bliss, experiments with LSD, and esoteric spirituality. Kosmische Musik's short history streaks like a soon to burn out comet across the discography cosmos, releasing albums by Ash Ra Tempel, Sergius Golowin, Walter Wegmüller, Klaus Schulze and Popol Vuh. When Kaiser resorted to the extreme measure of recording musicians in jam sessions by subterfuge and issuing their work under the Cosmic Jokers moniker, the label crashed and burned along with the remainder of the Kaiser's empire. The labels Cosmic Music and PDU released many of the great Kosmische Musik records in France and Italy respectively.

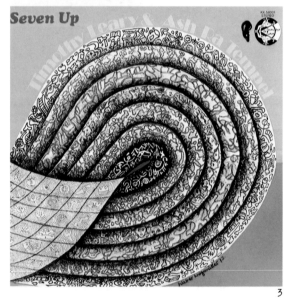

1 Kosmische Musik KM 58 001, 1972.

2 Kosmische Musik KM 58 009, 1974.

3 Kosmische Kuriere KK 58 001, 1972.

4 Kosmische Musik KM 58 002, 1973.

5 Kosmische Musik KM 58 013, 1974.

6 Kosmische Musik KM 58 008, 1973.

7 Kosmische Musik KM 58 010, 1974.

8 Kosmische Musik KM 58 016, 1975.

9 Kosmische Musik KM 58 011, 1974.

4

5

6

7

8

9

KUCKUCK

Founded in 1969 by Eckart Rahn, Mal Sondock and the advertising agency ConceptData in Munich, Kuckuck (aka Cuckoo Records) has the distinction of being among the very first "progressive" German record labels, as well as the longest surviving. Among its most notable releases were 1970's *Leere Hände* by Ihre Kinde (which inaugurated the label); *Wake Up* by Out Of Focus, in which rock song structures merged with jazz and melted into new psychedelic forms; and 1971's *D* by Deuter, whose innovative, multi-track guitars, flutes and electronics would eventually give way to a more conventional output of new age fare in the 1980s. Minimalist Terry Riley, a distant American touchstone for Krautrock, recorded for Kuckuck the two albums *The Descending Moonshine Dervishes* in 1982 and *Songs for the Ten Voices of the Two Prophets*, 1983, both featuring Between's Peter Michael Hamel. Eckart Rahn is currently based in Tuscon, Arizona, home of his new label (and Kuckuck distributor) Celestial Harmonies.

1 Kuckuck 2375 001, 1970.
2 Kuckuck 2375 004, 1970.
3 Kuckuck 2375 005, 1970.
4 Kuckuck 2375 006, 1970.
5 Kuckuck 2375 014, 1971.
6 Kuckuck 2375 003, 1970.

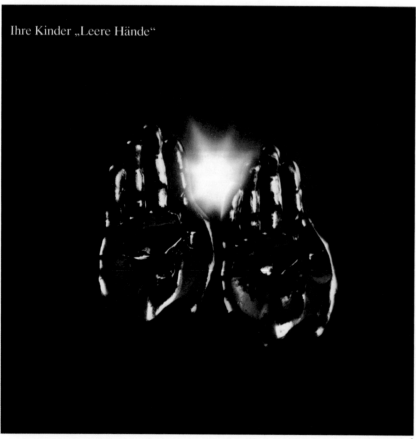

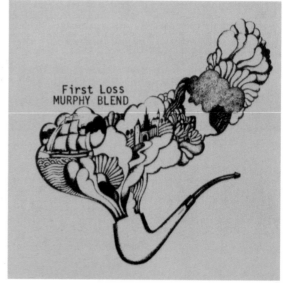

ARMAG
GEDON

4

Ernst Schultz
Paranoia Picknick

5

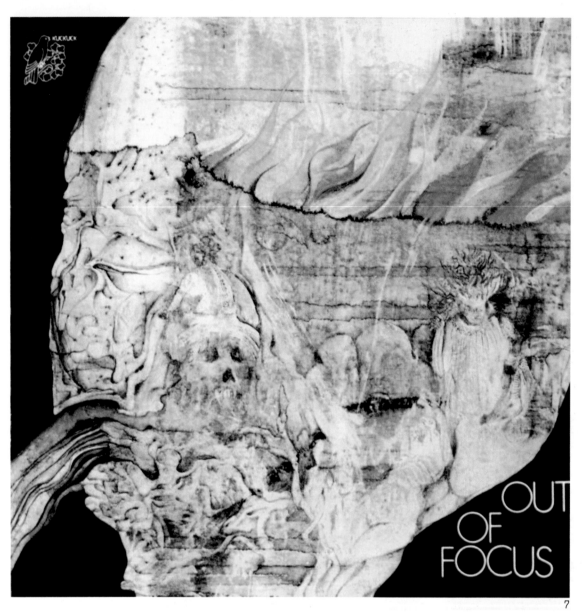

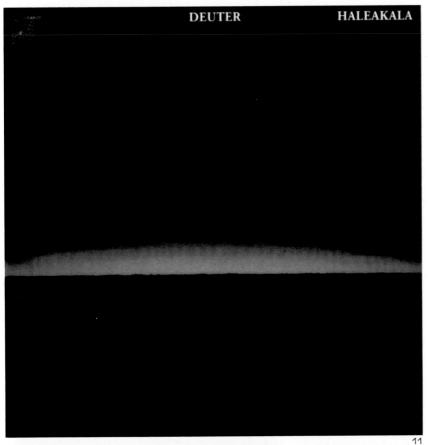

DEUTER   **HALEAKALA**

15

OUT OF FOCUS   FOUR LETTER MONDAY AFTERNOO

14

11

DEUTER
ECSTASY

12

Deuter   **Aum**

13

7 Kuckuck 2375 010, 1971.
8 Kuckuck 2375 011, 1972.
9 Kuckuck 2375 016, 1972.
10 Kuckuck 2375 022, 1973.
11 Kuckuck 2375 042, 1976.
12 Kuckuck 2375 017, 1972.
13 Kuckuck 2375 044, 1979.
14 Kuckuck 2640 101, 1972.
15 Kuckuck 2375 009, 1971.

OHR

Ohr (meaning "ear") records was founded in 1969 by Rolf-Ulrich Kaiser, out of his dissatisfaction with the conventional output of the record labels of his time. The previous year he had co-organised the festival International Essener Songtage and had begun writing his celebratory book *Das Buch der Neuen Pop Musik*, where he lamented the poor-sightedness of the music business and its neglect of the experimentation that Kaiser saw emerging worldwide. From its beginning right to its demise a few years later, Ohr went against any current or trend, becoming the first outlet for the sudden onrush of new German music, including names like Amon Düül, Floh De Cologne, Guru Guru and Tangerine Dream, many of whom had already appeared at Essen and other festivals organised by Kaiser. As well as the trademark ear on the label, the striking artwork by Reinhard Hippen featured, in the first five releases, the recurring motif of dismembered body parts, gracing the sleeves of Floh de Cologne's *Fliessbandbabys Beat-Show*, Tangerine Dream's *Electronic Meditation*, Bernd Witthüser's Lieder Von Vampiren, Nonnen und Toten, Embryo's *Opal*, and Limbus 4's *Mandalas*, signifying either the nascent and fundamental rearrangements of the new music, or eye-catching depravity, according to taste. Gil Funcius' designs for *Osmose* by Annexus Quam and *Trips und Träume* by Witthüser & Westrupp were equally striking. Prior to its abrupt collapse in 1974, Ohr's discography contained some of Krautrock's most inspired, if least commercial releases; it is gradually enjoying present day rediscovery.

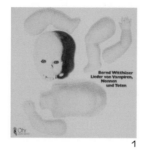

1

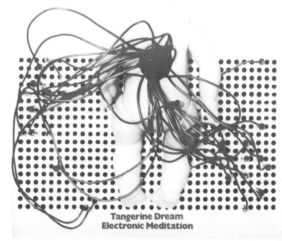

2

1 Ohr OMM 56002, 1970.
2 Ohr OMM 56000, 1970.
3 Ohr OMM 56004, 1970.
4 Ohr OMM 56001, 1970.
5 Ohr OMM 56003, 1970.
6 Ohr OMM 56005, 1970.
7 Ohr OMM 56007, 1970.
8 Ohr OMM 56010, 1971.

**Tangerine Dream
Electronic Meditation**

3

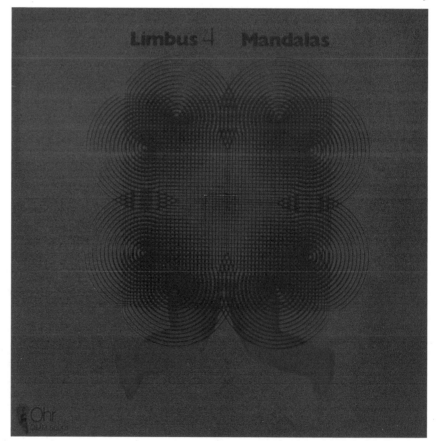

Limbus 4 Mandalas

4

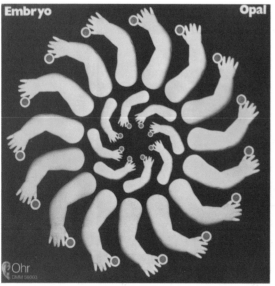

Embryo **Opal**

5

UFO

GURU GURU

6

7

ROCKOPER

FLOH DE COLOGNE

8

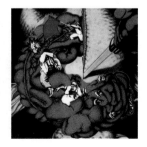

9

10

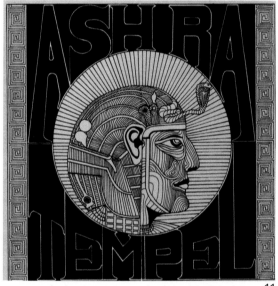

11

13

12

9 Ohr OMM 56011, 1971.
10 Ohr OMM 56012, 1971.
11 Ohr OMM 56013, 1971.
12 Ohr OMM 556020, 1972.
13 Ohr OMM 56016, 1971.
14 Ohr OMM 556017, 1971.
15 Ohr OMM 556033, 1974.
16 Ohr OMM 556032, 1973.
17 Ohr OMM 556022, 1972.

17

14

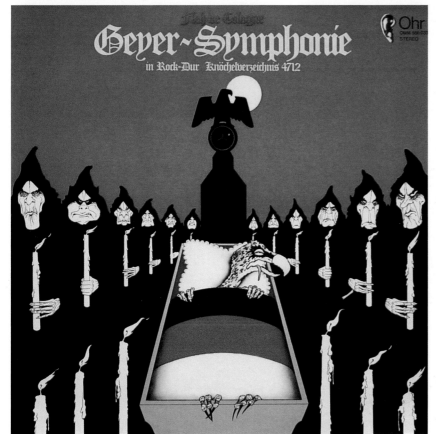

15

16

PHILIPS

Philips had been responsible for distributing the early white label logo releases of Bacillus. The giant label, founded by the Dutch electronics firm of the same name, would also be temporarily home to Cluster and Kraftwerk, while in 1970, they issued the legendary, dazzling, effects-laden triple album *Trip, Flip Out, Meditation*. Legend is that one of the producers at Philips was so enamoured with one of the female members of the group that he allowed them to record in the label's studios for free, after hours. This created a scandal and the album was deleted by Philips shortly afterwards, making it a much sought after item subsequently.

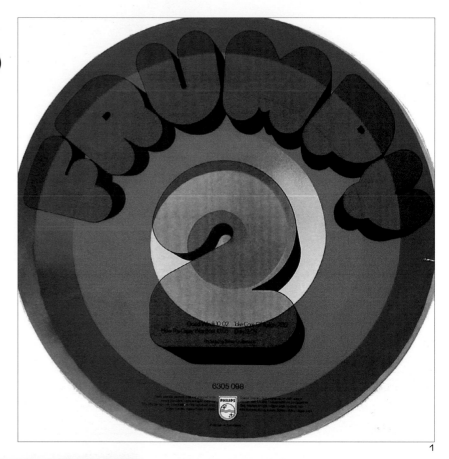

1

2

3

1 Philips 6305 098, 1971.
2 Philips 6305 074, 1971.
3 Philips 6305 055, 1970.
4 Philips 6305 127, 1972.
5 Philips 6305 095, 1971.
6 Philips 6305 067, 1970.
7 Philips 6305 128, 1972.

4

5

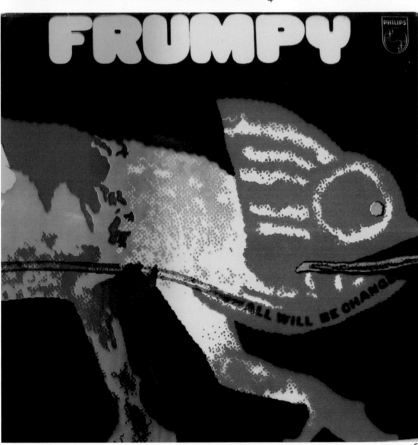

6

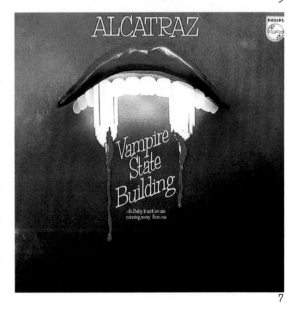

7

PILZ

In 1971, the major label BASF launched Pilz as a sublabel; in the same year they had released the Gila record *Free Electric Sound* and were eager to catch up with the German psychedelic scene. Jürgen Schmeisser, briefly appointed as a director, was almost immediately replaced by none other than Rolf-Ulrich Kaiser. Pilz represented both burgeoning underground activity and a more rustic, pastoral, folk-influenced output, reflecting Kaiser's own interest in the likes of Pete Seeger and Joan Baez. Among the most significant releases on the Pilz label were those by Popol Vuh, who acquired a wider audience thanks to their soundtrack work, and whose 1971 album In *Den Gärten Pharaos* was especially lauded. Other important releases included the Flute & Voice album *Imaginations of Light*, Emtidi's *Saat* and the first album by Bröselmaschine. Other artists, meanwhile, such as Witthüser & Westrupp, were sufficiently eclectic to put out material on both Pilz and Kosmische Kuriere. Pilz ceased its operations in 1973 after the release of Popol Vuh's *Hosianna Mantra*.

1 Pilz/BASF 20 21095-2, 1971.
2 Pilz/BASF 20 21088-2, 1971.
3 Pilz/BASF 20 21098-7, 1971.
4 Pilz/BASF 05 111101-0, 1971.
5 Pilz/BASF 20 21099-5, 1971.

4

5

1

2

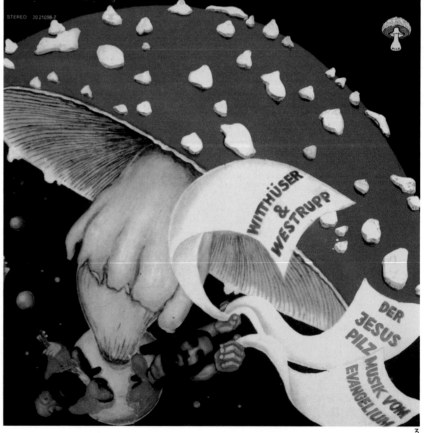

3

6 Pilz/BASF 20 29077-8, 1972.
7 Pilz/BASF 20 21103-7, 1971.
8 Pilz/BASF 20 21103-7, 1971.
9 Pilz/BASF 20 29115-2, 1972.
10 Pilz/BASF 20 29143-1, 1973.
11 Pilz/BASF 20 29097-2, 1972.

7

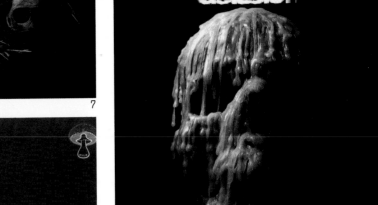

8

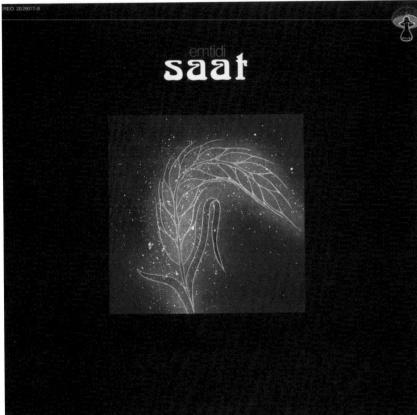

6

9

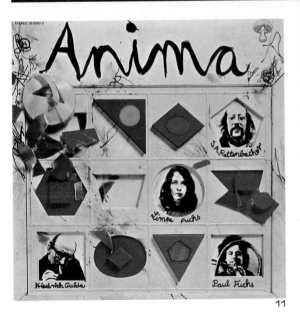

11

10

UNITED ARTISTS /LIBERTY

UA/Liberty was another major label with strong Krautrock connections, thanks to Gerhard Augustin, the former presenter of Beat Club. In the late 1960s, Augustin relocated to LA, and found work with United Artists, before returning back to Germany to continue working for the label there. The label, knowing very little of the German scene themselves but vaguely aware that something of interest was brewing there, trusted his insider knowledge and encouraged him to sign domestic acts. He was instrumental in signing up Amon Düül II, Popol Vuh and, significantly, Can, ensuring their wider dissemination and paving the way to their international recognition. The UA/Liberty/Krautrock interface wasn't always successful, however—the label picked up, then dropped, Embryo, whose particular take on jazz/rock didn't accord with the label's own preconceptions of either genre back in the early 1970s.

2

3

1

5

1 United Artists UAS 29 414, 1972.

2 Liberty LBS 83 342 I, 1970.

3 Liberty LBS 83 437 I.

4 United Artists UAS 29 505, 1973.

5 United Artists UAS 29 211/12 X, 1971.

6 United Artists UAS 29 239, 1971.

7 Liberty LBS 83 460, 1971.

8 United Artists UAS 29 781, 1976.

4

6

7

8

PRODUCERS

GERHARD AUGUSTIN

Courtesy Eurock Archives.

Gerhard Augustin is the bridge between the 'beat' and the Krautrock eras in German music. At a time when the country's scene was dominated by *schlager* (a German type of pop/folk music), he was among the few to play the new beat; always keen to embrace new sounds he went on to work with none other than the three quintessential Kraut bands Can, Popol Vuh and Amon Düül II.

In 1964, Augustin opened Twen, a discotheque/youth club in Bremen, becoming the city's very first German DJ. Having seen shows such as Shindig and Top Of The Pops while abroad, he mooted the idea of a German equivalent and The Beat Club, co-hosted by himself and Uschi Nerke, debuted on German television in September 1965. The Beat Club was the first German music programme to promote Anglo-American and German beat and rock music (including appearances by two leading German beat bands The Lords and The Rattles). The show's co-creator Mike Leckenbusch, eager to give Beat Club a more Anglo-American image, soon replaced Augustin with the British presenter Dave Lee Travis and switched the show to the exclusive promotion of British and US rock, inviting artists such as The Who, The Rolling Stones, The Beatles, Hendrix and The Small Faces. However, Augustin's connections, and his work as head of A&R for Liberty/UA records, enabled him to

attain some exposure for German bands, including Kraftwerk and Can, in the seventh and final year of the programme.

This is perhaps one of Augustin's most invaluable contributions—his continuous effort to promote as well as secure record label contracts for bands including Amon Düül II and Popol Vuh, and all of this in the face of establishment resistance ("some of the old Nazis were still in control of the media so they would never give exposure to new experimental rock music", Augustin told *Eurock*) and at a time when German bands were considered to have insignificant—if any—commercial appeal. That he convinced United Artists/Liberty to release an album as experimental as Popol Vuh's Moog-orientated debut *Affenstunde* (and this in 1969) is admirable indeed. Augustin went on to produce most of Popol Vuh's albums, but he also worked with famous international artists such as Ike and Tina Turner, Canned Heat and Shirley Bassey, and in the 1990s produced the three Amon Düül II albums *Live in Tokyo*, *Flawless* and *Kobe* (Reconstruction).

Augustin's vision and sheer love of music ("more important to me than sex, love or relationships", he has said) helped facilitate the maturity and worldwide dissemination of German music in the late 1960s and throughout the 1970s. Not for nothing is he known as the "Godfather of Krautrock".

DIETER DIERKS

Dieter Dierks with Embryo, during the production of *Embryo's Rache*. Courtesy Garden of Delights.

Dieter Dierks is best and somewhat depressingly known for bringing to the fore German heavy metal band The Scorpions, whose career he fostered from the mid-1970s onwards. Prior to that, however, he was, literally, instrumental in the development of Krautrock, playing with Ash Ra Tempel and the infamous group—who—had—no—idea—they—were Cosmic Jokers. He produced or engineered some of the most seminal Krautrock records ever including Tangerine Dream's *Alpha Centauri*, *Zeit and Atem*; Embryo's *Embryo's Rache*; and Floh de Cologne's *Geier Symphonie*.

Dierks was also involved in the Ash Ra Tempel albums *Schwingunen* and *7UP*, whose making was bathed in copious and discombobulating amounts of LSD, the world of "lysergic daydreams" in which the album was made. Dierks brought not only his abilities as a player and sound engineer but also a battery of synthesizers and echo-units in order to lend verisimilitude to the drug-induced soundworld created. It was Dierks' job to take the resultant, chaotic mess of recordings for *7UP*, involving countless vocalists and edit them down into something coherent in Berlin. He produced two later releases by Ash Ra Tempel, *Join Inn* and *Starring Rosi*.

Dierks ran the studios in which some of Krautrock's most extreme and insane odysseys into the druggy mystic took place, albums such as Walter Wegmüller's *Tarot*, Witthüser & Westrupp's *Trips und Träume*, Sergius Golowin's *Lord Krishna von Goloka*, and the sessions which gave rise to the Cosmic Jokers albums. Following the collapse of Ohr Records, however, and following his success in shepherding The Scorpions to superstardom, his career took a much more conventional turn, and the Dierks studios now resounded to the commercial metal sounds of, among others, Twisted Sister, The Plasmatics, and even big names such as Michael Jackson, Rory Gallagher, and Tina Turner who all recorded there.

ROLF-ULRICH KAISER

Rolf-Ulrich Kaiser (left) with Walter Wegmüller (right). Courtesy Walter Westrupp.

Rolf-Ulrich Kaiser is perhaps the most controversial, visionary, idealistic and ill-fated figures of the whole Krautrock era. Born in 1943, he began his career as a Dutch journalist working out of Cologne, and took a particular interest in the folk music scene, especially its countercultural aspect. He travelled widely to Europe and to America, interviewed Pete Seeger and Joan Baez among others, and, as is often the case with those who made the transatlantic journey, was inspired by visions of German musical self-sufficiency as a result. In 1968, he co-organised The Internationale Essener Songtage, a large festival in which the fledging likes of Amon Düül and Guru Guru played alongside overseas acts such as The Fugs, Julie Driscoll and Brian Auger. He also brought Frank Zappa and The Mothers Of Invention to Germany, a hugely significant event in Krautrock's development.

Kaiser founded the Ohr label in 1969, later followed by the labels Pilz and Kosmische Musik, while at the same time issuing a series of books, some of them concerning Frank Zappa. Hubris and Nemesis followed his involvement with Timothy Leary and the *7UP* sessions. He began to assume ideas of complete control, and to alienate artists, especially following the surreptitious recordings which gave rise to the Cosmic Jokers. However there is a counterargument that several of his artists, "moved on to sign bigger contracts, made good money, and became prolific artists who have had long careers. This was in no small part due to Kaiser giving them a start when they were free spirited youth. His knack for promoting his artists was innovative and

effective for those times." (Archie Patterson, "The Mythos of Rolf-Ulrich Kaiser", *Eurock*)

Hounded by lawsuits, threatened by musicians like Klaus Schulze and berated in the national press for his relationship with Timothy Leary, Kaiser was forced to abandon his musical interests, including his Kosmische Musik label, and disappear. To this day, no one really knows of his activities since, though rumours circulate that he is now dead. According to Klaus D Mueller, manager of Klaus Schulze and key player in the Berlin electronic scene, he lived for a while totally disillusioned and broke in Cologne, ruined and begging in the early morning hours for food with his wife Gille Lettmann. According to KDM, he was also officially pronounced schizophrenic, a result of his excessive LSD intake.

Kaiser's very high ambitions, his initial optimism and monumental attempts at creating and spreading a countercultural scene in tune with the worldwide underground, his gradual disillusionment with the music business (most evident in his final book *Rock Zeit*) and his tragic end parallel somehow the trajectories of both the musical and the political sensibilities of his time. By 1975, date of Kaiser's disappearance from the music business, the extra-parliamentary opposition was crashed by the alarming policies of the West German state, and state violence was escalating into what would eventually lead, two years later, to the events known as the German Autumn; Kaiser's disappearance also marked the end of the Krautrock era. A villain for some, his visionary, utopian spirit is still admirable to this day.

CONNY PLANK

Conny Plank (left) with Moebius (right). Courtesy Moebius.

Conny Plank (1940–1987) is a name so synonymous with Krautrock that he practically counts as a contributor rather than a facilitator. As with Kurt Graupner, sound engineer for Faust, it was his vivid sense of soundscape, as well as his innovative and technological wherewithal, which helped shape and colour the likes of Can, Harmonia and Cluster.

Plank provides an extraordinary link between German music past and present—he started working life as the soundman for Weimar siren Marlene Dietrich. In the late 1960s, he worked with Karlheinz Stockhausen and Mauricio Kagel, involved himself in the Cologne WDR studios and the burgeoning Berlin scene, and also engineered two important free jazz releases—Alexander Von Schlippenbach's *The Living Music* and Peter Brötzmann's *Nipples*. He went on to work with Kluster and Kraftwerk from their beginnings as Organisation up to and including *Autobahn*, as well as with Can,

NEU!, La Düsseldorf, Harmonia, and Guru Guru, with whom he also showed his skills as a musician. In 1972 he launched the short-lived Aamok, a label focusing on jazz rock, for which he produced the first and only record by Ibliss *Supernova*.

Plank brought to his work a crucial understanding of space, eschewing some of the more bombastic and stifling habits of 1970s production work. In this respect he was a key influence on Brian Eno in his Ambient series, as well as David Bowie on albums such as *Heroes*, whereon the Thin White Duke paid oblique homage to the methods of the producer. During the 1980s his reputation soared and the roster of artists with whom he worked became more international. Everyone from DAF, Echo & The Bunnymen and Eurythmics to Rita Mitsouko, and Ultravox availed of the Plank palette of production methods. He even turned down the opportunity to work with U2. Plank died relatively young, of cancer, aged 47 but his legacy is a colossal one.

Rudi Dutschke (centre) in a student sit-in, 1967. © bpk / Kunstbibliothek, SMB. Photo: Bernard Larsson.

TIMELINE 1967–1975

1967

• Formation of Tangerine Dream, Agitation Free, Manuel Göttsching's Steeplechase Blues Band and Klaus Schulze's Psy Free.
• Rolf-Ulrich Kaiser publishes *Das Song-Buch*, an overview of the international folk scene.
• Organisation of Essener Kabarett Festival, in which Floh de Cologne appear; it is a prelude to the major Essen event of the next year.

RECORDS
• Wolfgang Dauner *Free Action*
• Klaus Doldinger *Goes On*
• Soul Caravan *Get in High*

FILMS
• Volker Schöndorff *A Degree of Murder*
• Helke Sander *Break the Power of the Manipulators*

• Formation of Kommune 1 in Berlin. Some of its members will become close friends of Amon Düül, also forming this year. The Kommune gains legendary status through a combination of situationist provocations, scandals and a wide exposure in the national press. In April, upon the US Vice President's visit to Berlin, several of the Kommune's members are arrested, after a failed plan to attack him with "pudding, yoghurt and flour". As a result, the conservative publisher Axel Springer calls the members of Kommune 1 "communards of horror".
• The 26-year-old German literature student Benno Ohnesorg is killed in student demonstrations against the Shah of Iran's state visit to Germany. A turning point in German history, his murder triggers an expansion and radicalisation of the workers' and student movement throughout the entire country.
• In reaction to Ohnesorg's death Joseph Beuys founds "Deutsche Studentenpartei" (German Student Party).

Protest against the Springer empire.

1968

• Rudi Dutschke, central figure of the left-wing student movement is shot in the head but survives the assassination attempt. The incident triggers protest actions throughout West Germany against Alex Springer, whose conservative publishing empire is seen as instrumental in spreading hatred against the extra-parliamentary opposition movement and its leaders. Thousands of demonstrators unite in an attempt to block the delivery of Springer newspapers, including the popular tabloid *Bild Zeitung*.

• In an "act of political revenge", Andreas Baader, Gudrun Esslin, Thorwald Proll, and Horst Söhnlein set fire to two department stores in Frankfurt. The bombs explode at midnight causing considerable financial damage but no human casualties.

• The Bundestag passes the so-called Emergency Laws, in the face of the ever-increasing strong extra-parliamentary opposition. These laws curtail certain essential civic rights, in order to strengthen the capacity of the state to counter 'crisis' situations (revolution, war etc). Protests spread throughout the country, most notably in Bonn where 80,000 protesters gather in opposition.

• In August, Soviet tanks, reinforced by Polish, Hungarian and Bulgarian troops, roll into the Reform Communist Czechoslovakia of A Dubcek.

• Documenta IV opens in Kassel, featuring a selection of Minimal, Conceptual and Kinetic Art. Some of the exhibition's conservative opponents describe it as a "modern house of horrors". The exhibition features a performance by Amon Düül.

• The activist Beate Klarsfeld publicly slaps the Chancellor (and ex-Nazi) Kurt Georg Kiesinger in the face; while being pushed away by security she is heard shouting "Kiesinger! Nazi! Abtreten!" ("Kiesinger! Nazi! Step down!").

• Formation of Can and Guru Guru Groove.

• The International Essener Songtage, "a festival with politics, art and pop" following the example of Monterey in California, opens in September, hosting a diverse list of international and German acts, including Tangerine Dream, Floh De Cologne, Guru Guru, and The Mothers of Invention. The subtitle "Deutschland Erwacht" (Germany Awakens) is adopted as an ironic, provocative twist of a nineteenth century nationalist motto. A key, formative event for the burgeoning Krautrock scene, the music festival is also a platform for countercultural activity, discussion and debate, with concerts often ending in conversations with the audience. In one of the festival's most notorious performances, Floh de Cologne include pornographic slides and finish their set by inviting the audience to squat and steal basic food provisions from shops, this earning them legal proceedings for blasphemy and procuration.

• Zodiak Free Arts Lab is founded by Conrad Schnitzler, Hans-Joachim Roedelius and Boris Schaak in Hallesches Ufer, Kreuzberg, Berlin. Though only lasting for a few months and eventually closing in 1969, the Zodiak gains legendary status and sees performances by Klaus Schulze, Agitation Free, Human Being, Eruption as well as the first incarnation of Tangerine Dream. A wild and eclectic mix of free jazz (Peter Brötzmann, Alfred Harth, Irene Schweitzer, Sven Ake Johannson would all play there), improvisation, psychedelic rock and avant-garde fills the performance spaces with destruction of the equipment often closing a set. In its considerably brief life span, the Zodiak deeply resonates with the events taking place outside and forges an unparalleled unity of art, politics and noise. The later RAF member Holger Meins, Bommi Baumann—a young construction worker and a later key figure of the organisation Movement 2 June—and Karl-Heinz Pawla are amongst its regular guests.

Eruption at the Zodiak. Photo: Werner Strey.

RECORDS
- Bokatz Retsiem *Psychedelic Underground*
- Floh De Cologne *Vietnam*
- Stockhausen *Stimmung*
- Wolfgang Dauner *Requiem for Che Guevara*
- Peter Brötzmann *Machine Gun*

FILMS
- Hellmuth Costard *Besonders Wertvoll*
- Werner Herzog *Signs of Life*
- Alexander Kluge *Artists Under the Big Top: Disorientated*
- Klaus Lemke *Negresco*
- Holger Meins(?) *Herstellung eines Molotow-Cocktails*
- May Spils *Go for it Baby*
- Jean-Marie Straub and Danièe Huillet *The Bridegroom, the Comedienne and the Pimp*
- Rudolf Thome *Detektive*
- Wim Wenders *Same Player Shoots Again*

Essener Songtage poster, 1968. Courtesy Deutsches Plakat Museum. Photo: Jens Nober.

• Formation of Popol Vuh, Kluster and Embryo.

• The Zodiak closes its doors after members of the revolutionary, proto-terrorist group Zentralrat der Umherschweifenden Haschrebellen (whose university teach-ins often feature performances by bands such as Tangerine Dream and Agitation Free) set fire to a police car in reaction to the frequent drug raids undertaken at the club.

• Liberty/United Artists, under the efforts of A&R director Gerhard Augustin, release *Monster Movie* by Can and *Phallus Dei* by Amon Düül II.

• Rolf-Ulrich Kaiser publishes *Das Buch der Neuen Pop Musik;*, the first of his books to speak enthusiastically about the new German music scene, it covers Tangerine Dream, Can, Xhol Caravan, Limbus, Embryo and Floh de Cologne. Kaiser links German rock to a countercultural, underground scene emerging worldwide. Kaiser's driving idea is that it is possible to overcome capitalism by building structures that are independent, non commercial and countercultural. The same year also sees the publication of two other books by Kaiser: *Underground? Pop? Nein! Gegenkultur! Eine Buchcollage* and *Fuck the Fugs—Das Buch der Fugs.*

• The label Kuckuck is created by Eckart Rahn.

• The last ever Burg Waldeck festival is held in September and features appearances by Xhol Caravan and Tangerine Dream. It marks a departure from the singer/songwriter element of the previous five years.

• Rolf-Ulrich Kaiser and Peter Meisel found Ohr Records. Until its demise in 1973, the label releases a total of 33 albums by names such as Tangerine Dream, Amon Düül, Klaus Schulze, Ash Ra Tempel, Witthüser & Westrupp, Popol Vuh, Floh De Cologne, Guru Guru, Embryo and Anima. Its first release is *Fliessbandbabys Show* by Floh de Cologne.

• American President Richard Nixon visits Berlin. Rainer Langhans and Dieter Kunzelmann, are falsely accused of attempting to bomb Nixon's motorcade when a bomb, planted by notorious police spy and agent provocateur Peter Urbach the day before Nixon's arrival, is found in the premises of Kommune 1.

• Willy Brandt succeeds Kiesinger as Chancellor of West Germany and remains Head of Government until 1974; his chancellorship marks a cultural change in the political affairs of the Federal Republic.

• Kombinat 1, a Fluxus commune and exhibition space is founded in Cologne by the composer Mauricio Kagel, Wolf Vostell and others.

• Uwe Nettelbeck (Faust's producer) publishes an article in *Zeit* on the trial of Red Army Faction member Andreas Baader which results in a tough warning from the magazine's editor.

• Publication of the notorious Rolf-Dieter Brinkmann book on the American counterculture *ACID. Neue Amerikanische Szene*, a collage of texts by William Burroughs, Michael McClure, Frank O' Hara, Taylor Mead, Ted Berrigan and others.

RECORDS
• Amon Düül *Psychedelic Underground*
• Amon Düül II *Phallus Dei*
• Peter Brötzmann *Nipples*
• Can *Monster Movie*
• Limbus 3 *New Atlantis*
• Organisation *Tone Float*
• Alexander von Schlippenbach *The Living Music*
• Xhol Caravan *Electrip*
• Wolfgang Dauner *Oimels*

FILMS
• Peter F Schneider *Agilok & Blubbo*
• Rainer Werner Fassbinder *Love is Colder than Death*
• Rainer Werner Fassbinder *Katzelmacher*
• Rudolf Thome *Rote Sonne*
• Volker Schlöndorff *Michael Kohlhaas—Der Rebell*

1970

- Formation of Ash Ra Tempel.
- Conrad Schnitzler leaves Kluster; Cluster in born.
- Karlheinz Stockhausen represents Germany in the World Fair Expo '70 in Osaka, Japan. In a spherical auditorium designed by Stockhausen, 20 instrumentalists perform his compositions for more than a million listeners over the course of three months.
- Love-and-Peace open air festival organised in Insel Fehmarn in which Jimi Hendrix gives his last ever performance. Alongside Hendrix, the last day of the festival features performances by Witthüser and Westrupp, Embryo, Floh de Cologne, Limbus 4 and an embryonic version of Ton Steine Scherben. While Scherben perform their song "Macht kaputt, was euch kaputt macht" ("Destroy what Destroys You") the stage is set on fire and the festival ends in chaos. Riots are spreading backstage by unpaid workers while the organisers attempt to leave the festival pocketing all the profits.
- The Petards, a beat 1960s band, organise the festival Burg Herzberg featuring Amon Düül, Gila, Can, Tangerine Dream, Guru Guru and Limbus.

- The SDS (Sozialistische Deutsche Studentenbund) disbands. This date marks the gradual 'disintegration' of the student movement into conflicting and opposing factions.
- Wolfgang Huber, a young psychiatrist working at Heidelberg University gets fired due to his radical therapy methods. In response to his firing, Huber's patients occupy the offices of the hospital's director; the Socialists Patients Collective (SPK) is born. Some of its members later join the Red Army Faction.
- Andreas Baader is freed from prison with the help of Ulrike Meinhof, an event that marks the formation of the Red Army Faction.
- The "Happening and Fluxus" exhibition opens in the Neuer Kölnischer Kunstverein gallery, in Cologne, presenting a documentation of about 500 happenings from the years 1959–1970.

RECORDS
- Amon Düül *Paradieswärts Düül*
- Amon Düül II *Yeti*
- Annexus Quam *Osmose*
- Can *Tago Mago*
- Wolfgang Dauner *Output*
- Embryo *Opal*
- Floh De Cologne *Fliessbandbabys Beat-Show*
- Guru Guru *UFO*
- Organisation *Tone Float*
- Kluster *Klopfzeichen*
- Kraftwerk *Kraftwerk 1*
- Popol Vuh *Affenstunde*
- Tangerine Dream *Electronic Meditation*
- Xhol *Hau-Ruk*

FILMS
- Werner Herzog *Even Dwarves Started Small*
- Hans-Jurgen Syberberg *San Domingo*
- Rainer Werner Fassbinder *Niklashausen Journey*
- Rainer Werner Fassbinder *Warum Läuft Herr R Amok?*
- Wim Wenders *Summer in the City*

SOLIDARITÄT MIT DER ROTEN ARMEE FRAKTION!
FÜR DEN AUFBAU DER STADTGUERILLA!

RAF

1971

• Michael Rother and Klaus Dinger leave Kraftwerk and form NEU!.

• Rolf-Ulrich Kaiser 's Pilz label is founded. Main artists: Popol Vuh, Virus, Hölderlin, Wallenstein, Dies Irae, Joy Unlimited, Witthüser & Westrupp. Ceasing its operations after two years, the label releases a total of 20 albums.

• Gunter Körber and Bruno Wendel leave Ohr due to possible disagreements with Rolf-Ulrich Kaiser to set up their own label Brain Records. The most prolific of all Krautrock labels, Brain releases all three NEU! albums, as well as records by Guru Guru, Cluster, Harmonia, Edgar Froese, Embryo, Thirsty Moon, Eroc, Yatha Sidra and Popol Vuh.

• Eurock, a Californian two-hour radio show is aired for the first time, soon followed by a fanzine with the same name. It features music by AD II, Popol Vuh, Can and many others. In its prolific 20 year life span, the fanzine will become one of the main US Krautrock sources of information.

• Bacillus Records founded by Peter Hauke, with Dieter Dierks as the main engineer for almost all of the records released.

• Willy Brandt receives the Nobel Peace Prize for his Ostpolitik—an effort to improve relations with East Germany, Soviet Union, Poland and other Eastern Bloc countries.

• Movement 2 June, named after the date of Benno Ohnesorg's death, is formed in Berlin by previous members of Kommune 1.

• Ulrike Meinhof's manifesto "The Concept of the Urban Guerilla" achieves wide circulation. Its cover is adorned with a rifle over a star with the letters RAF (Red Army Faction) written on top of them.

• The Tory government expels Rudi Dutschke and his family (who were then seeking refuge in Britain) on the grounds that Dutschke was an "undesirable alien" who has engaged in "subversive activity".

• A remarkable poll is published, revealing that one in five Germans under 30 expresses a certain sympathy for members of the RAF.

RECORDS

• Amon Düül II *Tanz der Lemminge*
• Ash Ra Tempel *S/T*
• Deuter *D*
• Embryo *Embryo's Rache*
• Faust *S/T*
• Floh de Cologne *Rockoper Profitgeier*
• Guru Guru *Hinten*
• Kluster *Zwei Osterei*
• Kraftwerk *Kraftwerk 2*
• AR & Machines *Die Grüne Reise*
• Tangerine Dream *Alpha Centauri*

FILMS

• Rainer Werner Fassbinder *Beware of a Holy Whore*
• Rainer Werner Fassbinder *Whity*
• Werner Herzog *Fata Morgana*
• Volker Schlöndorff *Sudden Wealth of the Poor People of Kombach*

1972

Courtesy bpk.

• Willy Brandt passes the so-called Radikalenerlass or Anti-Radical Decree. Under this law, the state had the authority to disqualify certain employees working in the public sector, if they held radical left-wing ideals or any sympathy for the Red Army Faction. As a result, 3.5 million individuals are investigated and 10,000 refused employment. The Decree is a final, decisive blow to the already torn extra-parliamentary opposition.

→ Amidst the glory and spectacle of the Munich Olympics, members of the Palestinian organisation "Black September" capture Israeli hostages in the Olympic village.

• *Der Spiegel* publishes a letter by future Nobel laureate Heinrich Böll, in which he accuses Springer's newspaper *Bild* of "naked fascism, agitation, lies, dirt".

• Documenta 5, one of the most legendary exhibitions of the twentieth century opens under the direction of Harald Szeemann with the title "100 Days of Inquiry into Reality—Today's Imagery". Documenta features works by over 170 artists and an equally expansive variety of materials and subjects drawn from popular culture.

• Joseph Beuys dismissed from Kunstakademie Düsseldorf. Amongst the reasons for his dismissal was his earlier decision to abolish entry requirements to his class.

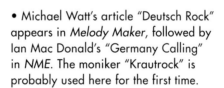

• Michael Watt's article "Deutsch Rock" appears in *Melody Maker*, followed by Ian Mac Donald's "Germany Calling" in *NME*. The moniker "Krautrock" is probably used here for the first time.

• Kaiser replaces Ohr with the label Kosmische Musik. He organises several recording sessions with members of Wallenstein, Witthüser and Westrupp, Klaus Schulze, Manuel Göttsching and Harmut Enke, followed by the release of Ash Ra Tempel's *7UP*. The label is Kaiser's last. His last book *Rock Zeit*, a book about "stars, business and history of pop music" is also published this year. A certain pessimism permeating the book sets it apart from his earlier euphoric views of the counterculture. The same year that the foreign press documents the 'Krautrock explosion', Kaiser talks of German rock as already disintegrating into a commercial venture, turning away from the experimentation of the previous years.

RECORDS
• Agitation Free *Malesch*
• Amon Düül II *Carnival in Babylon*
• Ash Ra Tempel *Schwingungen*
• Ash Ra Tempel *7UP*
• Can *Ege Bamyasi*
• Cluster *II*
• Deuter *Aum*
• Dzyan S/T
• Faust *So Far*
• NEU! S/T
• Conrad Schnitzler *Rot*
• Klaus Schulze *Irrlicht*
• Tangerine Dream *Zeit*

FILMS
• Werner Herzog *Aguirre the Wrath of God*
• Hans-Jürgen Syberberg *Ludwig*
• Hans-Jürgen Syberberg *The Merchant of Four Seasons*
• Wim Wenders *The Goalkeeper's Fear of the Penalty*
• Volker Schlöndorff *Die Moral der Ruth Halbfass*
• Volker Schlöndorff *Strohfeuer*

1973

• Ash Ra Tempel and Xhol Caravan disband.

• *Actuel*, a French underground magazine with a situationist ethos, publishes a two-part article on the German counterculture including "Le Rock Allemand, Enfin!" ("At Last! German Rock has arrived!"). A festival is curated in Paris in February of the same year, including Kraftwerk, Guru Guru, Tangerine Dream and Ash Ra Tempel, most of whom give their first ever performance in France; it also features the first solo appearance of Klaus Schulze. The sold-out festival is a triumph and marks the beginning of the French success of Tangerine Dream, Manuel Göttsching and Klaus Schulze.

• Pilz ceases operations. The last record released is Popol Vuh's *Hosianna Mantra*.

RECORDS

• Agitation *Free Second*
• Amon Düül II *Wolf City*
• Ash Ra Tempel *Join Inn*
• Ash Ra Tempel *Starring Rosi*
• Manuel Gottsching *Inventions for Electric Guitar*
• Can *Future Days*
• Dzyan *Time Machine*
• Exmagma S/T
• Faust *Faust Tapes*
• Ralf & Florian S/T
• NEU! *NEU!2*
• Popol Vuh *Hosianna Mantra*
• Conrad Schnitzler *Blau*
• Klaus Schulze *Cyborg*
• Tangerine Dream *Atem*

FILMS

• Alexander Kluge
Gelegenheitsarbeit einer Sklavin
• Wim Wenders *The Scarlet Letter*

• Agitation Free disband.

• Metamusik, an avant-garde and ethnological 'world' music festival is organised in Berlin's Nationalgalerie, featuring performances by Terry Riley, Peter Michael Hamel, Steve Reich, Peter Glass and Alvin Curran.

• During a collective hunger strike by the main members of the Red Army Faction that results in the death of Holger Meins, philosopher Jean Paul Sartre interviews Andreas Baader in the Stammheim prison, after a request by Ulrike Meinhof.

• Willy Brandt forced to resign as Chancellor after it is revealed that Günter Guillaume— one of his closest aides—had been working for the Stasi. Brandt is succeeded by Helmut Schmidt who adopts a tough policy in extinguishing West German terrorism.

• Heinrich Böll publishes *The Lost Honour of Katharina Blum or How Violence Can Develop and Where It Can Lead*, a commentary on the political climate of panic over the wave of terrorism and a fierce critique of the sensationalism of right-wing tabloid press.

1975

• Virgin rejects the fifth album by Faust; the band disbands shortly thereafter.
• Günter Körber leaves Brain and founds Sky Records, a label carrying the Kosmische and Krautrock flame well into the early to mid-1980s. It will be home to Asmus Tietchens, Michael Rother, Moebius and Plank, Cluster and many others.
• Ridiculed in the national press and hounded by lawsuits against his publishing and music empire RU Kaiser disappears. Kosmische Musik comes to an end.

• Bommi Baumann publishes his autobiography Wie alles anfing ("How it all began") which is seized by the police immediately after its appearance because of its supposed incitement to violence.
• Peter Lorenz, CDU candidate for Berlin mayor is kidnapped by members of the Movement 2 June. In exchange for his release four of their imprisoned comrades are released. Following their example, six members of the Red Army Faction occupy the West German Embassy in Stockholm, demanding the release of RAF prisoners.

RECORDS

• Amon Düül II *Vive La Trance*
• Can *Limited Edition*
• Can *Soon Over Babaluma*
• Cluster *Zuckerzeit*
• Faust *Faust IV*
• Harmonia *Musik von Harmonia*
• Kraftwerk *Autobahn*
• Klaus Schulze *Black Dance*
• Tangerine Dream *Phaedra*

FILMS

• Rainer Werner Fassbinder *Ali: Feat Eats the Soul*
• Rainer Werner Fassbinder *Effi Briest*
• Wim Wenders *Alice in the Cities*
• Hans-Jürgen Syberberg *Karl May*
• Werner Herzog *The Enigma of Kaspar Hauser*

RECORDS

• Stockhaseun *Tierkreis*
• Can *Landed*
• Harmonia *Deluxe*
• Kraftwerk *Radio Activity*
• NEU! *NEU!'75*
• Klaus Schulze *Timewind*
• Tangerine Dream *Rubycon*

FILMS

• Volker Schlöndorff and Margarethe von Trotta *The Lost Honour of Katharina Blum*
• Rainer Werner Fassbinder *Fox and his Friends*
• Rainer Werner Fassbinder *Mother Küsters' Trip to Heaven*
• Wim Wenders *The Wrong Move*

AT LAST: GERMAN ROCK HAS ARRIVED!
JEAN-PIERRE LANTIN

ACTUEL NO. 27, PARIS: NOVAPRESS, JANUARY 1973. TRANSLATION BY CLODAGH KINSELLA, 2009.

The stage is plunged in semi-darkness, a projector casting a faint glow over three musicians sitting behind three organs. Sprouting out of their instruments, like a jungle of charged plants, the mishmash cubes of VCS3 synths, echo chambers, tape recorders, ring modulators and white noise generators. This is a music that unfurls with slow solemnity: electronic variations on a single note that continue for an hour, unbroken. "Kosmische Musik", it's called. The band is Tangerine Dream, one of Germany's oldest. Six years ago, clad in tight English-style suits and pussybow collars, they were playing the Kinks and Rolling Stones. But Berlin in 1968—a hotbed of radical politics, communes, LSD and heroin—launched them towards more heady climes. Awash with radical new sounds and given over to freeform improvisation, it gave birth to this tranquil, dreamlike sound. A more precise and minimal operation than ever, over the last year Tangerine Dream have become, paradoxically, what one might call a "commercial success".

Amon Düül II are another group just surfacing from hectic times. Never having flirted with traditional rock music, they launched themselves wholeheartedly into sonic revolution. Five years ago, all the members of their commune—musicians and non-musicians, adults and children alike—took to making wild music devoid of any tonality or the least concession to regular beat. Some of the group went on to join forces with Berlin's Kommune I, launching a sporadic, madcap musical collaboration under the name Amon Düül I. Amon Düül II, in contrast, followed a very linear path towards traditional rock: after three albums of breathless improvisation, the two last ones, *Carnival in Babylon* and *Wolf City*, were dedicated to sumptuous composition and finely-honed recording techniques. Given over to full and silvery Baroque harmonies, the records profit from an extraordinary palette of bizarre timbres and electronic effects. Legendary in their native land, Amon Düül II (the commune has since disbanded), have just finished their second UK tour and are breaking out Europe-wide.

In 1969, two members of the contemporary music scene created Can—proving that the great musical shake-up wasn't about to spare Stockhausen's disciples either. Professional pianist Irmin Schmidt took things back to scratch and played nothing but one solitary note for days on end. Much to his surprise, music teacher Holger Czukay morphed into a pop musician, seizing hold of the bass because "it's an instrument that no one listens to, so you can do whatever you want with it". Jacqui Liebezeit, the former free jazz drummer, went to great lengths to simplify his playing and ensure the message got through. Today Can are one of Germany's most popular groups, despite never having adulterated their sound.

For Tangerine Dream, Amon Düül II and Can, as for other established German bands, the period of heroics is at an end. They have all accomplished the great 'clear up', the tabula rasa. These days they are maturing and working on new things, setting up solid foundations for the decade to come.

Mani Neumeier has a wild and lined face, skin drawn taut against his skull and a sulphurous gleam in his eye. The two tips of his well-kempt moustache frame his mouth like Fu Manchu. Although addled by drug trips and the nervous energy of his music, he's still got plenty of life left in him. As a member of Guru Guru, for the past five years he has been playing acid music with its anarchic bent and apocalyptic electric style. When they perform, the band set up their amps at the front of the stage so that the music assaults the audience's eardrums, locking horns with them like some rampaging beast and reining down a hail of body blows. Mani Neumeier (drums) and Uli Trepe (bass), the two founders, were formerly in a free jazz ensemble; guitarist Ax Genrich counts Hendrix as an influence. Between the three of them, they perform two-hour sets of furious improvisation, so tireless and unstoppable that they spend more than 200 days a year on the road. "Acid, as a revolution, is over. The public isn't interested anymore. The time of small clubs, intimate circles of initiates banding together to get high, is in the past. These days we play large halls with a lot of young kids of 14 or 15, drinking beer. There was a stage when we were caught off-guard, we who essentially played 'stoner music', but we've got used to it." Mani Neumeier is now 31; Uli, who left the group several months ago, is 30. Guru Guru have just finished mixing their fourth album in Hamburg. They've refined and restrained the improvisation, without completely embracing structure. It's reminiscent of the last Miles Davis records, with their alternations and tessellated rhythms—a stream of electric planes interspersed with weird and hoarse spoken word vocals. "Instead of permanent aggression we've adopted humour. People can still have fun within the confines of the system." Holed up for several days in a luxury hotel in one of Hamburg's chicest quarters, Guru Guru still seem a bit shell-shocked by their lavish surroundings. Not far from here, their producer Conny Plank has a superb three-storey house that also functions as the base of Aamok, the record label he recently founded.

With 150 signed bands and 200 albums released by German groups in 1972, German rock is now big business. In 1970, one journalist, Rolf-Ulrich Kaiser, founded the first label devoted to German bands. These days all the big companies have sub-brands that operate according to this model (Brain, Spiegelei, Zebra, Harvest, Made in Germany). There's even frequent critique of the glut, each label recording 20 groups on the off-chance that two or three will break through. Dull imitations of English fashions abound. We won't speak of them here—they're just sickly offshoots. The German scene still

gives out strong vital signs. Undeniably, though, instead of the tumult that plucked musicians from all different backgrounds and piled them into a great melting pot, the scene has now cloistered itself into non-communicative currents. "Polit" or "agit"-rock is one example: only the most hardened remain, but they have several successes to their credit. Once or twice a year, Floh de Cologne put on booming satirical shows in all the major German towns, attracting crowds a hundred thousand-strong and largely made up of young disciples. The latest one, *Lucky Strike*, told the story of a workers' strike. Ton Steine Scherben, a band based in Berlin, are firm fixtures at the parties and demonstrations. Theirs is a basic rock music, "something that ordinary people can get to grips with"—their lyrics even more populist, but delivered with a seemingly unshakeable revolutionary zeal. They've made two albums off their own backs, completely outside of the system, and sell them for less than the usual retail prices. Following their example, other committed groups are producing their own albums, groups like Hotzenplotz and Comcol.

German law prohibits managers: most groups, whether they like it or not, take the business end of things into their own hands and deal directly with promoters, putting on their own gigs and generally banding together. The idea of the popular group or "people's band" still dominates the scene. A band like Faust, launched as a "supergroup" to huge PR fanfare, were greeted by critical and public approbation, much like Jürgen Dollase, the frontman of Wallenstein, was considered a bit too much the "pop star". Yet

at the same time, it's not rare for bands to publish their own underground fanzines—the members of Bröselmaschine regularly edit *Der Metzger*—or engage in open collaborations, ready to support any likeminded initiative (Lord's Family, Out of Focus, Annexus Quam).

Germany has held onto a pronounced taste for experimentation after its five years of musical anarchy. The ten groups referenced here aren't exhaustive of the whole German rock scene, but they're more or less the most eminent ones in the country. They represent the best that Germany has to offer, slowly overthrowing all the crusty pillars of rock and contemporary music and, almost alone in the world, making the music of the decade to come.

One by one and in a deep voice the words fall slowly from his lips, his eyes often drifting vacantly towards the ceiling. An emaciated but smiling face. "I'm so tired. This year we've made two albums, taken a lot of substances". Hartmut Enke is 20, having dropped out of school three years ago to found Ash Ra Tempel, one of the first bands to have played the Berlin sound. Berlin—the monster of cities where all the cracks in the social fabric, drugs and student revolts collide more violently than anywhere else in Europe. Berlin—exhibiting itself in opulent displays but trapped, isolated and hermetically-sealed by the East German border. Berliners don't just flit off for weekends or whole weeks in the country: it takes five to seven hours on the motorway just to get back to West Germany. It's impossible for a band to follow a normal schedule or to play as much as two or three gigs a year in Berlin. So the musicians play for each other, deepening their experiences, turning inwards. For several months in 1969, everyone went to the Zodiak, the Berlin equivalent of Ufo or Paradisio: the musicians and their audience bound together by the token of psychedelic drugs. In the backroom one could hunker down in an armchair, observe the Berlin metro through the porthole windows or let the mind wander as the world went by.

Ash Ra Tempel got together there, uniting the old drummer from Tangerine Dream with two blues' musicians, Harmut Enke and Manuel Göttsching. Before long the blues was lost in the upheaval, replaced by long improvisations around rhapsodic monotones, musical flats like a beach at low tide, with all the brash rhythms and electric discharges of rock carried away on receding waves. In their place, a chastened ripple that hankers after the slow cycles of meditation—an invitation to close your eyes and dive into the soft swaying of slumber.

Yet Ash Ra Tempel have almost never played this blissed-out music live. Disorganised by principle and by cult of spontaneity, they play to a serendipitous rhythm—withdrawing to private studios in the company of whichever musicians chance their way. The projected release date of their third album is the beginning of 1973. Recorded with Timothy Leary, it also features him offering advice in an enigmatic and enlightened whisper atop the ethereal vibrations of musicians in full-on trip mode. Last autumn the group splintered yet again—Hartmut and Manuel now left to conduct the hunt for a new bassist and drummer. They returned to Berlin a month ago but it seems more like a couple of days. They wander about their

half-empty apartment, take in the old baroque furniture and wall-hangings with the spaced out demeanour, faint voices and faded gestures of zombies, only venturing 20 metres down the road to grab a pizza when midnight comes. "Berlin musicians are attached to the city, they can't leave it. We've liberated ourselves from all that this summer. Now we can go anywhere. There's no scene left in Berlin, nothing to do here—except die." They hope to set themselves up in the country, Switzerland maybe. "The other day we entered a room where Tangerine Dream were playing—we were flipped out by the sinister atmosphere which was so disturbing that after five minutes we just left. We want to do something else—not completely abandon electronic music, but give good vibrations, play happy songs, a bit of blues maybe."

Tangerine Dream's riposte: "Ash Ra Tempel live in a dream world. They think that everything will turn out okay, that the expansion of consciousness will conquer the world and all the problems will solve themselves. We try and be more realistic: the expansion of consciousness is just one part of reality and misery and horror are another part that you can't ignore." Tangerine Dream's music is even more laidback and ecstatic than Ash Ra Tempel's, but also more sombre, a bit lugubrious: the sound of organs stretched out inordinately, solemn harmonies that collapse one into the other or, like on their last album *Zeit*, one note extending over all four sides, a unique murmur without melody or concession save the subtle modulation of waves and timbres. "Each side of the record should last an hour. We need ten minutes or so just to get into the music. After that,

things really get started." Edgar Froese, the only original band member left, is a man as slow and heavy as his music. Chubby of face, his stomach is rotund and his beard red and bushy. At opposite poles to Ash Ra Tempel, he lives with his wife and daughter in a modern apartment filled with "design" furniture. The three members of Tangerine Dream all went to university and constitute the conscious, intellectual contingent of Berlin "kosmische musik". Whilst Ash Ra Tempel get most of their effects from acoustic instruments, Tangerine Dream surround themselves with mountainous amounts of electronic gadgetry. Yet like most of the German musicians who have made the journey from rock to electronic, the band were scarcely versed in the developments of the contemporary music scene—Stockhausen, Cage and all the "experimental music laboratories". Even today they deny their legacy: "I mostly listen to classical music. I try and recreate the feeling of classical but using modern acoustic instruments."

The same concern motivates Klaus Schulze, former member of Tangerine Dream and Ash Ra Tempel, who is now pursuing a solo career as an electro-acoustic musician. He's not a "composer" but an improviser, an artisan. He refuses the cosmetic enhancements of tape recordings, prefers 'live' broadcasts and playing in public so as to get instant feedback and make modifications accordingly. For his first album, *Irrlicht*, Schulze engaged 29 musicians from a Berlin symphony orchestra: "I want to keep hold of the sounds of classical instruments where you feel the tangibility of the wood or metal and not get too attached to the overly 'pure' sounds of electronic music. It's not right to completely lose touch with classical music—it's our education and our heritage. Instead it's better to find a way to combine all different types of music."

"We recorded in a room at the Berlin Free University, using my portable mini-studio. First of all it took me a whole evening just to explain to them that I wanted one note, beginning very softly, then little by little reprised by the whole orchestra over the space of the next ten minutes. They tried but at once got carried away. I described to them the fascination of monotony, of repetition. Nothing doing. I had to write a score. Then I asked them to improvise—they felt completely out of their depth. When I announced that I was going to record the strings the right way round and the brass backwards, they broke out in high-pitched shrieks. It's just as well that I didn't mention my intention to process the whole thing through a wah-wah and a ring modulator."

Klaus Schulze declares himself unsatisfied, but the results are spectacular: a great shimmering blanket of organ and synthetic sound with far-off Wagnerian echoes, like some funerary march in space.

"I went into a shop one day and said: I want that, that and that, I'll put it on credit. That's how I got my equipment. I never paid for anything. I've got the police on my tail". Conny Schnitzler looks nothing like any of the other Berlin musicians. The antithesis of those placid youths, he's all sparks, speaking quickly and jumping from one topic to another amid frequent bursts of laughter. Involved with Tangerine Dream back in 1969, he tried—without success—to push them towards a pure electro-acoustic sound, while at the same time manning his own group, Eruption. "Tangerine Dream were supposed to be playing at Essen festival alongside several well-known Anglo-Saxon bands. The public were really just coming to see them, and would probably take the mickey out of the other bands they hadn't even heard of. So I proposed that they come on naked except for leather aprons and make a hell of a racket with hammers, anvils and a forge. They strenuously refused. My second idea was to get ten flippers and hook them up to the frequency modulators in the hope of producing some sound and also to get the audience to have a go on them. Rejected. Third idea: to set up the equipment and walk off stage, leaving the amps to blast constant feedback. Rejected. So that's why I left Tangerine Dream."

The following year he formed Kluster, engaging two other musicians and then ditching them. Ever since, he has produced his own work under the name Kluster I. We caught up with him in a Hamburg museum where he was manning one of the rooms in the exhibition Berlin '72. "I hate being here, I'm only doing it because I need the money, but it's definitely the last time. Museums are dead places full of dead people. I like playing in normal places—discos, big rooms like Fabrik, rock concerts: you have to play your best and get people on your side or you get kicked off." Shaven headed, with the thick moustaches of a suave Taras Bulba, and little eyes that wrinkle as he lights upon each new idea, Schnitzler is without doubt one of the most invigorating musicians in Germany. "I've only got my electric instruments on me right now, it's a pity, I'd have liked to show you my violins—I give them to other people to play, show them how. Everyone ought to be able to play music. But all my violins are broken."

Conny Schnitzler represents an alternative to Tangerine Dream and Klaus Schulze, finding their way of doing things too formal and too rigid. He likes uninterrupted concerts of 12 or 24 hours ("The public can come and go, listen to snippets as they please"), wants to make new synth plug-ins which would allow anyone—in return for a financial contribution—to play a complex piece of electronic music and take the recording home as a souvenir. He always remains a few years ahead of his compatriots, scattering new ideas and then moving on to something new. Cluster II, the duo he formerly worked with, have moved from Berlin to Hanover where their music is harder and more aggressive than the Berlin bands: infernal bellows which pour from one channel of the stereo into the other—groaning and muted explosions which alternate and sit alongside the slow and hypnotic cycles of "kosmische musik".

The Munich region—a sort of Teutonic San Francisco with a more southern and nonchalant vibe, has given birth to the latest school of "cosmic music"—Georg Deuter and the two musicians who make up Popol Vuh. No classical music, a gentler and more joyful pace than the Berliners, with the presence of the sitar, tabla, oriental flute and acoustic guitar. Georg Deuter has travelled around India and picked himself up a guru (no money changed hands, he makes sure to add). He practices yoga and meditation. "All my compositions are built on a counterpoint I sourced from Indian music, and which acts on the listener as a calming gravitational pull. By renouncing the primitive rhythms of rock and introducing sounds taken from the environment, the music no longer allows itself to be consumed as a product, but instead as a conscious creation." Recorded at home, Deuter's music is a collage of myriad soothing morcels; bits of sitar and acoustic guitar, pipes, electronic hisses, the sound of water or birds and the lax percussive rhythms of India—a music meant for meditation.

On Popol Vuh's records, similarly, one side will often open and close with the sounds of water, while Turk or African percussion keeps up a sensual and soporific pulse. Florian Fricke, his curly hair framing an aquiline face, is the sole German to use one of the big Moog studio synthesizers. His sonic experiments have led him on a wild and unexpected ride: "I came to yoga through the synthesizer. I was a Marxist before. I started to get into the theoretical physics of vibration and it was there that I encountered religion." To compose music on the Moog necessitates, according to Fricke, an action that is conscious and responsible. No sound is neutral, for all modify consciousness and perception: the idea being that through reflection, intuition and the study of oriental music, comes the recognition that music has the power to heal, fulfil and take the listener on a journey through inner space. Unlike Deuter's music, the colourful sounds of Popol Vuh are sometimes intense—almost fit to burst, as in "Vuh", where

majestic swells emanate from the depths of a church organ, the power of their waves washed out by cymbals.

More than any other German artists, Deuter and Popol Vuh have distanced themselves from the idea of a rock or pop music. Infused with oriental influences, they reject in equal measure the hardcore Bach and Wagner-philes who still linger on the Berlin scene, proposing a new take on the western musician as doctor, magus or shaman.

Bern Brummbär, the easy-going editor of Frankfurt underground paper *Germania*, nicely captures the attitude of most of the "cosmic" musicians—their total rejection of the aggressive: "I shrink from a brutalist aesthetic, from these arrogant ideas of western musicians. They always want to get people to 'wake up'. Here, musicians are very polite, very humble. They only care about God and their music. They want to produce something well made, an object of beauty."

Fortunately there are still a few German groups left practising the "brutalist aesthetic". Can, for example: drums that mercilessly shell the listener like a great steam engine sputtering coal, organ and guitar submitted to shock treatment and Damo, the Japanese singer, dreaming up over-the-top characters to play—a crazy mandarin, an overwrought Italian impresario or soliloquizing Shakespearean actor. There's Kraftwerk too: brittle mechanised rhythms, great washes of wild electro-acoustics that echo off industrial noise as reactors roar, steelworks and furnaces resound and there come the screams of crushed sheet metal. NEU! have a track called "Negativland"—a guitar solo

ripped up by distortion, tones corroded as though by acid—like Giacometti's sculptures made sound. Faust, too: a blackly comic music; biting, nightmarish. This last group comes from the industrial capital, Hamburg, the three others from the Ruhr—that great constellation of cities scored by motorways emitting an acrid stench like old coal engines as they rip through the tunnel's confines. They play the music of big cities, hunger after violence—aggression as a weapon against an aggressive society—and don't stray too far from rock and its brutal stop-start rhythms. "We completely refuse to make a judgement about what is beautiful and what isn't. We make something, that's all, and the scope of possible sounds is just immense. We're not musicians, we're universal dilettantes. The biggest danger for German musicians is to want to become another Stockhausen—a serious musician, an artist. To want to create beautiful things, to have good taste, to keep in the back of your mind this idea of perfection." Holger Czukay, the bassist of Can, looks a bit like an idiot savant with his great black coat and unruly locks just beginning to grey around the edges. Now and then the mischievous smile hints at some ulterior motive. He studied for three years with Karlheinz Stockhausen, the supreme pioneer of contemporary German music. Irmin Schmidt, the organist, also spent a year with him. "Stockhausen is a good composer, and a very wise man, but he's a man of the nineteenth century. Before I joined the band I thought about mining a similar path but today I know that I will never be able to go back to that again. Times have changed." The Can experience began five years ago without any fixed ideas. They still don't have a plan today, which is precisely what provides the group with its potency and strength. Can never play exactly the same piece twice; they improvise and record in their own studio every day, extracting bits here and there to make up their albums. The last one, *Ege Bamyasi*, is more laid-back, warmer than the previous ones. The band has been listening to Miles Davis; the drums have softened up. On stage, it's different. "You need to have a rhythm which stops people thinking. The other instruments can do what they want, but the rhythm has to be unremittingly strong." There, too, don't bother trying to recognise a familiar, fleeting refrain: it's all a matter of improvisation again.

Kraftwerk live and play for the night. The band are pale, you would almost think them creatures of the night or even vampires. Ralph Hütter sports a black leather number with white boots, his hair tied back in a ponytail. Flegmatic and taciturn, for the last month he has lived in a large, empty apartment that he hasn't taken the trouble to furnish: white walls, mattress on the floor, an eerie echo to every room. Around midnight he goes out to hook up with Florian Schneider-Esleben in a private studio. They are the two founders of the group, together again after a number of adventures. Both of them studied classical music but have long since shrugged off the bonds of the old model. They play the flute, the violin, guitar and organ, systematically warping conventional sounds with new ways of playing or electronic effects. They've carefully listened to Terry Riley, the principle of repetition—short musical phrases which imperceptibly change. Droning drums and the mechanical rhythms of a drum machine rock their improvisations with hypnotic symmetry. Sometimes the music becomes completely atonal—the pure fascination of noise; clinking, grating. To their name they have two of the most experimental—and two of the bestselling—albums to come out of German rock.

Curious overlaps and analogous musicians link Kraftwerk to NEU!. Another duo from Düsseldorf, Klaus Dinger and Michael Rother are also both multi-instrumentalists. Their sound is more electronic, their beats more regular than Kraftwerk. "Music doesn't take off without the pulsing beat of rock. I don't think much of the so-called genius of machines. Together Ralph and Florian have tried to do without rock, to produce electronic sounds without rhythm. They gave up. No one could understand them anymore. Rock is a way of getting to people. It's hard for someone leading your average modern life to listen to electronic music". They added a bassist and a drummer for gigs. They gave that up, because they didn't recognise themselves anymore. For the moment they've abandoned playing live, refusing an English tour in February 1973. In Germany, this kind of integrity is no longer surprising. Klaus Dinger recently shaved his head and now resembles a Martian. In white overalls with bare feet and bracelets looped around his ankles, he comes to pick us up in a vast, gleaming Mercedes. A cassette tape of the band comes over the stereo as the car slips silently through the deserted Düsseldorf streets at two in the morning. The décor perfectly suits this acid lament, at the same time melancholic and euphoric—the nightly music of ultra-modern cities, peopled by ghosts: plate-glass windows, illuminated signs, traffic lights, lifeless chromium façades.

"If you know any good French groups who aren't recording, tell them to send me their demos. Nothing much is happening in Germany you know, it's hard to find musicians who aren't just making servile copies of Anglo-Saxon stuff—who have a style that's really original." Can it be that Conny Plank is joking? He himself has produced Guru Guru, Kraftwerk, NEU! and Cluster II. But now he complains about being unable to find new and interesting groups for his label. In 1972, banal rock made a big comeback amongst young musicians. Some people are already having doubts about the changing of the guard. Yet Walpurgis, a new Berlin band, have just undergone a startling reversal: after an album of classic rock songs, they've moved on to improvisation, and for several concerts—maybe more—Conny Schnitzler has set them up with his electronic equipment. Rolf-Ulrich Kaiser, the producer of the Berlin "cosmic" groups, receives demos from young bands aping Tangerine Dream on a weekly basis. In Germany today many take to imitating electronic music in the same way that they copied Led Zeppelin four years ago. There's still time for some exciting discoveries before German rock degenerates into mere formulaic clichés.

CONTRIBUT

ERIK DAVIS

is a San Francisco-based writer, culture critic, and independent scholar. He is the author, most recently, of *The Visionary State: A Journey through California's Spiritual Landscape*, and he also penned a short critical volume on Led Zeppelin's fourth album. His book *TechGnosis: Myth, Magic, and Mysticism in the Age of Information* has become a cult classic of visionary media studies, and has been translated into five languages. Davis has contributed to scores of magazines and books, and has taught at UC Berkeley, UC Davis, Pacifica, the Maybe Logic Academy, and the California Institute of Integral Studies. Some of his work can be accessed at www.techgnosis.com.

MICHEL FABER

is a novelist and short story writer, whose books include Under The Skin, *The Crimson Petal and the White*, *The Fire Gospel* and *The Fahrenheit Twins*. He also reviews music-related books for *The Guardian*.

KEN HOLLINGS

is a writer based in London. His work appears in a wide range of journals and publications, including *The Wire*, *Sight and Sound*, *Strange Attractor* and *Frieze* and in the anthologies *The Last Sex*, *Digital Delirium*, *Undercurrents* and *London Noir*. His novel *Destroy All Monsters* was hailed by *The Scotsman* as "a mighty slab of trippy, cult, out-there fiction, mind-bending reading". He has written and presented critically acclaimed programmes for BBC Radio 3, Radio 4, Resonance FM, NPS in Holland and ABC Australia. His latest book, *Welcome to Mars: Science and the American Century 1947-1959*, is available from Strange Attractor Press.

DAVID KEENAN

is an author and critic based in Glasgow, Scotland. A contributor to *The Wire* since 1994, Keenan has also written for *NME*, *Melody Maker*, *Uncut*, *Mojo*, *Ugly Things*, *Opprobrium* and *The Sunday Herald*, where he was the resident jazz critic in the early 2000s. He is the author of

England's Hidden Reverse, a secret history of esoteric art and music in the UK and the co-owner of Volcanic Tongue, a mail order and record shop that specialises in underground music. He digs Walter Wegmüller and Conny Veit the most.

STEVE KRAKOW (AKA PLASTIC CRIMEWAVE)

has been carrying the Midwestern psychedelia/ Krautrock/spacepunk/acid-folk/etc torch for a number of years. He regularly performs with bands Plastic Crimewave Sound, Moonrises and DRMWPN; writes/draws the "Secret History of Chicago Music" comic strip; curates the Million Tongues festivals; freelances for a number of publications; DJs across the US; and is also known as the editor/creator of psychedelic culture magazine *Galactic Zoo Dossier*.

BRIAN MORTON

has been a university teacher, newspaper journalist, broadcaster, musician and farmer. He presented jazz and classical music on BBC Radio 3 and for ten years his own daily live arts programme on BBC Radio Scotland. His books include nine editions of the *Penguin Guide to Jazz* (eight of them with the late Richard Cook), *Contemporary Composers*, *In Search of Eden*, and books on Miles Davis, Shostakovich and Prince. He now divides writing with running a small croft in the west of Scotland. His saxophones are in genteel retirement.

LEON MURAGLIA

discovered Kraftwerk and DAF in his early teens and his true love: electronic music and hence, synthesizers. Working in various London venues through the 1990s he was a founder of Kosmische club, which, with a team of DJs, became a regular event in London and has now spread to Oslo and FM radio, with sporadic events around the UK and many European cities. He now resides in Oslo, Norway, with his girlfriend and small collection of synthesizers, where he composes, plays in the band Radio 9, DJs and is currently making a feature documentary film about Krautrock.

OR BIOS

ARCHIE PATTERSON

began Eurock in 1971 as a prime time California radio show on a commercial FM station, which was followed by the first issue of *Eurock* fanzine in March 1973 covering music by Popol Vuh, Tangerine Dream, Can and other Krautrock artists. In the future, Eurock will focus on audio and video podcasting as well as features and interviews utilising the latest tools and avenues of exposure now made available via the internet. *Eurock: European Rock and the Second Culture*, a 700-page anthology of almost all the articles that have appeared in the fanzine, was published in 2002. More info at www.eurock.com

MARK PILKINGTON

is a London-based writer, publisher and musician. He runs Strange Attractor Press, home of *Strange Attractor Journal*, *Medical London*, *Welcome to Mars* and other fine books, and its CD label, Further. When not squinting at words, he can be found coaxing sounds from circuits with musical outfits including Disinformation, Raagnagrok, Oort, Yan-Gant-Y-Tan and The Asterism. More info at www.strangeattractor.co.uk

GAVIN RUSSOM

was born in 1974 in Providence, Rhode Island, HP Lovecraft's "universal haven of the odd, the free, and the dissenting". As an artist and musician he has pursued a singularly focused set of visionary aesthetics, goals and states across a wide range of media. His work, which often borders on the mystical, first came to public attention through his seven-year collaboration with Delia Gonzalez. The duo built installations and listening spaces that blurred the lines between art, ritual and entertainment and released the epic "El Monte" 12" single and the album *The Days of Mars*. In 2006 Russom's focus shifted to solo work and most recently he has performed as Black Meteoric Star, a project named after a celestial object and god figure from Pawnee Indian mythology. The debut self titled Black Meteoric Star album was released in the summer of 2009 by DFA Records, accompanied by three separate 12" singles.

ANN SHENTON

has been a member of Add N to (X) and is currently co-running White Label Music, an independent label based in Windsor, UK. She has used Theremins, moogs, Gestaposizer, banjo, dogs and sheep to create her signature sound. Since 2003 she has been recording under the name Large Number, and has released the album *Spray on Sound*, and the 7" EP "The Now Defunct Delaware". A new mini-album, *Modern Horror*, is due for release soon.

DAVID STUBBS

is a music journalist and author, who has written for *The Wire*, *The Guardian*, *NME*, *Melody Maker*, *Uncut* and *The Sunday Times* among others. He is also the author of *Fear Of Music: Why People Get Rothko But Don't Get Stockhausen*, published by zer0 Books.

STEPHEN THROWER

is a musician, author, film writer and member of London act Cyclobe. He has collaborated with Coil on the albums *Scatology*, *Horse Rotovator*, and *Love's Secret Domain*, was a former member of Skullflower and Possession and has appeared in Derek Jarman's *Imagining October*, *The Last of England* and *Caravaggio*. His first book, *Beyond Terror: The Films of Lucio Fulci*, was published in 1999, followed by *Eyeball Compendium*, 2003, and *Nightmare USA: The Untold Story of the Exploitation Independents*, 2008.

ACKNOWLEDGEMENTS

Our gratitude to the following people for their generosity, advice and support; without their help this project would be impossible:

Eckart Rahn/Celestial Harmonies, Alan and Steve Freeman, Steve Larkin, Olivier Bégué, Christian Piednoir, Armin Theissen, Johannes and Bettina Fricke, Dolf Mulder, Andrew Liles, Gérard Nguyen, John Higgs, Brian Barritt, David Robb, Michael Hoenig, Heidi Ramseier, Michael Rother, Detlev Mahnert, Mani Neumeier, Conrad Schnitzler, Roedelius, Moebius, Klaus Unland, Eberhard Kranemann, Christian Burchard, Rob Young, Eroc, Hildergard Schmidt, Sandra Podmore, Stockhausen Foundation, Stadtarchiv Essen, Bildarchiv Preussischer Kulturbesitz, Hendrik Boxberg/Museum Folkwang, Antje Pfeffer/Archiv der Jugendkulturen, Limpe Fuchs, Seven Legged Spiders & Co, Peter Thomas, Werner Herzog Film Office, Historisches Museum Frankfurt Am Main, Christina Bolius/Photography of the Rhine Art Scene, Museum Kunst Palast, Eva Engelberger/Museum Moderner Kunst Stiftung Ludwig Wien, Deutsches Plakat Museum, Rudolf Thome, Avo Raup, Miki Yui, Walter Westrupp, Dan Wilson, Jeannette Roth/tarotgarden. com, Solandia/aeclectic.net, Dick Städtler, Stephen Iliffe, Hans Brandeis, Raül Jordi/Wah Wah Records, Matthias Thiel/German Cabaret Archives, Richard Langston, Garden of Delights, Leon Muraglia and the Kosmische team.

A very big thank you to Clodagh Kinsella for the attentive and laborious translation of the French article by Jean-Pierre Lantin and to the kind staff at Novapress, Paris, for the permission to reprint it.

Thank you to Johanna Bonnevier whose design pushed the book to a totally different level.

Thanks also to Ulrich Klatte/the Cosmic Price Guide book, John Hubbard, Gareth Goddard, Jarrod, and Ed Pinsent for their help with record covers; to Steve Stapleton for his early involvement; to Wolfgang Seidel and Archie Patterson for their enthusiasm, critical input and for providing some of the most mind-blowing images from the times; to Mark Pilkington whose advice and support helped shape the book from the earliest stages and to David Stubbs for patiently accommodating our often unreasonable requests.

Extra special thanks to David Keenan, Erik Davis, Gavin Russom, Steve Thrower, Ann Shenton, Steve Krakow, Brian Morton, Ken Hollings and Michel Faber for accepting to be part of this book and for their invaluable contributions.

Edited by Nikolaos Kotsopoulos at Black Dog Publishing.
Designed by Johanna Bonnevier and Matthew Pull at Black Dog Publishing.

Band Profiles by David Keenan, David Stubbs, Brian Morton, Archie Patterson, Leon Muraglia and Mark Pilkington.
Record Labels/Producers by David Stubbs.

Cover artwork from *We Keep On* by Embryo. Used with permission of Christian Burchard.

Black Dog Publishing Limited
10a Acton Street
London WC1X 9NG
United Kingdom

ISBN 978 1 906155 66 7

British Library Cataloguing-in-Publication Data.
A CIP record for this book is available from the British Library.

Black Dog Publishing Limited, London, UK, is an environmentally responsible company. *Krautrock, Cosmic Rock and its Legacy* is printed in Malta by Melita Press on an FSC certified paper.

architecture art design
fashion history photography
theory and things

black dog publishing

www.blackdogonline.com   london uk